Project Management for Banks

Project Management for Banks

Dan Bonner

BUSINESS EXPERT PRESS Q

Leader in applied, concise business books

First published in 2021 by
Business Expert Press, LLC
222 East 46th Street, New York, NY 10017
www.businessexpertpress.com

ISBN-13: 978-1-63742-111-6 (paperback)
ISBN-13: 978-1-63742-112-3 (e-book)

Business Expert Press Portfolio and Project Management Collection

Collection ISSN: 2156-8189 (print)
Collection ISSN: 2156-8200 (electronic)

First edition: 2021

10 9 8 7 6 5 4 3 2 1

Description

Project management processes have been intertwined within every fabric of human evolution including advances in communication, farming, construction, medicine, law, architecture, physics, and economics to name a few. At each evolutionary stage, there was a project manager who was studying the how and why of everything, trying new techniques, and documenting trials, errors and successes until a specific craft was mastered, thrusting progress forward in an upward trajectory that has been carved into human history.

There are countless books and articles that focus on the practice of project management. What makes this book different is the focus placed largely on the project management processes for United States (U.S) bankers. This book starts with a look at the historical progression of project management processes but quickly focuses the material on project management processes for bankers, heavily leaning towards project managers in U.S. banks. The book also looks at the bank regulatory agencies that govern U.S. banks, regulations critical to the U.S banking system, and concludes with an overview of U.S. banking technologies and the management of a U.S. banking customer call center.

The book provides a comprehensive perspective on the U.S. banking project management processes, the regulatory agencies that govern and influence those processes, how technology, and more specifically, the development and use of artificial intelligence, will create a shift in the evolutionary trajectory of U.S. banking practices, and how U.S. banking project management practices will be at the core of how quickly and how successfully this evolution unfolds.

Keywords

project management; banking; federal reserve; waterfall project management; agile project management; U.S. Bank Regulations; U.S. Bank Regulatory Agencies

Contents

CHAPTER 1

The History of Project Management

Prostitution may be infamous as the oldest profession in the world but I would argue it is project management. If we use the definition of project management from the Project Management Institute as, "the application of knowledge, skills, tools, and techniques to project activities to meet the project requirements" (www.pmi.org) and the definition of a project as, "a temporary endeavor undertaken to create a unique product, service, or result" (www.pmi.org), evidence can be found in the Book of Genesis, King James version of the Bible that God used basic project management principles to create the heavens and the earth. As God was creating the heavens and the earth, first creating light and separating light from darkness through the creation of the seas, all plant life, all animal life, and human life, God used a work breakdown structure, or "project to do list" (www.apm.org.uk) of all things that needed to be created to support life. It was clear he had a project plan in mind when he decided to first create light, then earth, then the seas, until finally creating man in his image. At each step of the process, he is monitoring and controlling his own work, as only God can, by evaluating what he has created and deciding, "it was good." Lastly, the project satisfied the requirements of being a temporary endeavor as God finished on the sixth day and rested on the seventh. As such, project management could be not only the oldest profession in the world, but quite possibly the very first.

Chapter 1 presents an in-depth historical perspective on the evolution of project management from the earliest periods of time through the present. Such an in-depth look is required to fully understand how human evolution contributed to project management evolution: everything from advances in communication, farming, architecture, building, material gathering and usage, and execution. All of the factors built on one another until we finally arrive at modern day project management, arguably brought to fulfillment in the twentieth century. Having that in-depth knowledge provides a foundation to build upon much like executing any well thought project management plan.

Beginning with ancient civilizations, this chapter will review the history of project management from highlighting the social, economic, and scientific factors that most influenced the development and progression of project management over time; provide insight into the life of Frederick Taylor and his impact on the study and implementation of modern project management, how the publication of *The Principles of Scientific Management* impacted industries both domestically and globally, Henry L. Gantt's invention of the "Gantt chart" that improved time and motion studies, and how project management has progressed in the twentieth century and beyond.

Project Management in Ancient Civilizations

The foremost authority on the history of project management is Y. C. Chiu, whose books include,

> *An Introduction to the History of Project Management: From the Earliest Times to A.D. 1900, A History of Ancient Project Management from Mesopotamia to the Roman Empire, A History of Medieval Project Management: From the Byzantine Empire to the Gothic Period, and A History of Modern Project Management: From the Renaissance to the Machine Age.*

All books were published by Eburon Academic Publishers in 2010, 2011, 2012, and 2013 respectively.

Y. C. Chiu begins his analysis in the first known civilization of Mesopotamia around 10,000 years ago "because it is thought to be where human civilization first settled into a sedentary way of life" (Chiu 2010). Mesopotamia was located between the Tigris and Euphrates Rivers, "which are now the modern nations of Iraq, Iran, Turkey and Armenia" (Chiu 2010).

Chiu points out that the earliest settlers in the area were hunter-gathers. However, people began to experiment with grains in the area and successfully began growing food. This development provided an opportunity for people to stay in one place for longer periods as there was a consistent supply of food without having to rely on the variability of hunter-gathering techniques for sustenance. The ability to stay in one place sparked, "numerous developments not known to have previously existed" (Chiu 2010). These developments include the first known form of writing, which spawned the basis for government with rules and regulations, religious beliefs, architecture, and even basic bookkeeping that created the foundation for economic progress.

The impact it had on project management was that by documenting materials used, procedures for building and farming, successes and failures, settlers archived "how to" manuals that got passed on for analysis and updating. Over time, improvements were made in farming, building, mathematics, science, and astronomy but none more important to the population than in the areas of construction. Dwellings that were once made of marsh reeds were now being built with mud brick, creating a reinforced structure. The population grew as reinforced structures allowed for people to live in stable homes near sustainable food and water supplies, and ultimately taking the shape of towns and cities as mortality rates decreased.

As populations increased, there was a need for further development to feed and house people more quickly. After the wheel was invented by Mesopotamians around 3,500 BC, the world was forever changed. The wheel allowed for mass quantities of resource gathering such as wood, stone, and metals, which contributed to the speed and efficacy at which a structure could be built. After the invention of the wheel came the invention of the ramp, which then led to the construction of multilayered structures, the Hanging Gardens of Babylon being one of the more famous. It is believed that "the gardens were a tiered structure built on stone foundations with brickwork above and layers of reeds and bitumen (bitumen was used as a type of mortal between bricks and stones)" (Chiu 2010). Without the invention of the wheel and ramps, construction of these structures was not possible.

These structures could not have been built without a project manager or managers. However, at that time, there was no such role as a project manager but a "master builder." A master builder would have been knowledgeable in areas of architecture, engineering, and building. For large projects like the pyramids, a work breakdown structure was created where the master builder would oversee all operations and delegate responsibilities to those specialized in a specific aspect of the project be it architecture, engineering, or building.

As time went on, developments continued to be made in areas of language, writing, government, economics, medicine, philosophy, and construction. The advent of shipping via waterways and increase in overall travel brought ideas to and from shores all over the world. This not only spurred the transportation of materials but also the refinement of construction methodologies. As such, the ability to construct massive structures was first being seen in Greece, Italy, and China and then escalating into massive projects all over the world. As time went on, project managers who once oversaw simple dwellings in the areas of Mesopotamia were now overseeing such complex structures as the Great Pyramid of Giza, the Great Wall of China, the Parthenon, the Colosseum, St. Peter's Basilica, the Taj Mahal, right through to the transcontinental railroad and the Empire State Building. It was not until Frederick Taylor wrote *The Principles of Scientific Management* in 1911 that the role of the project manager broadened from architects and builders to every conceivable industry worldwide.

Frederick Taylor: *The Principles of Scientific Management*

Frederick W. Taylor (Taylor) was born on March 20, 1856, to Franklin Taylor, a prominent lawyer at the time who grew substantial wealth with mortgages, and Emily Annette Taylor (née, Winslow), "a vocal proponent of women's rights and vigorous opponent of slavery" (Wren 2011; p. 13). Wanting to walk in his father's footsteps, Frederick Taylor applied for Harvard Law School and passed all entrance exams with honors. However, due to rapidly deteriorating eyesight, Frederick Taylor pursued a different path working first as an apprentice with several companies including Enterprise Hydraulic Works and Midvale Steel as he had a strong penchant for understanding and detailing processes and procedures.

It was during these apprenticeships that Taylor observed a type of behavior he called "soldiering", which in its simplest form could be described as underachieving, but the more complex explanation is "when paid the same amount, workers will tend to do the amount of work the slowest among them does" (Taylor 1911). After obtaining his bachelor's degree in mechanical engineering from Stevens Institute of Technology in 1883, Taylor was committed to conducting scientific research that would explain the "motives that influence men" (Taylor 1911; p. 119). He felt that if done properly, aligning monetary incentives to the completion of tasks would improve employee productivity and eliminate soldiering altogether.

In 1886, Taylor joined the American Society of Mechanical Engineers (ASME) where he attended a presentation by then ASME president, Henry R. Towne, on "The Engineer as an Economist." Towne advocated that an "Economic Section" be created within the ASME to educate the individual engineer on economics since the combination of a good engineer and a good businessman is "essential to the management of industrial works, and has its highest effectiveness if united in one person who is thus qualified to supervise, either personally or through assistants, the operations of all departments of a business, and to subordinate each to the harmonious development of the whole" (Towne 1886). Towne referred to this as "Shop Management and Shop Accounting," which influenced Taylor to focus his attention on the economic forces impacting the advancement of the business as a whole regardless of the industry or establishment. Taylor then began to formulate and publish his own ideas on "time study to eliminate wasted motion, set an appropriate standard of performance, pay for performance, worker selection and training—and the mutual interests between workers who wanted high wages, and the manufacturers who wanted low costs..." (Wren 2011, pp. 14–15). In 1903, Taylor published his first book, *Shop Management*, which "was a handbook for managers, not an academic presentation, and placed the responsibility on management to do a better job of setting standards, selecting and training, providing incentives, and recognizing the shared interests they had with their employees" (Wren 2011, p. 15).

Shop Management as well as other early Taylor publications garnered him global recognition as a pioneer of improved efficiency in the workplace.

Starting in 1907, Taylor had a reputation of creating efficiencies in the workplace, bridging employee and management relations, and conserving of natural resources. While some took exception to these principles, particularly members of the ASME that Taylor was now president of, Taylor pressed forward with his ideals. He was holding discussions at his house in Chestnut Hill, Pennsylvania, which were well attended by those looking to better understand and implement Taylor's ideas. In attendance was Morris L. Cooke, whom Taylor hired as a stenographer to record the talks. Cooke's intention was to edit the talks and publish a book of his own, *Industrial Management*, from the material grounded in Taylor's discussions. However, Taylor was working on publishing what would become his most notable publication, *The Principles of Scientific Management* that would have conflicted with Cooke's book. After a somewhat minor controversy where Taylor was accused of plagiarizing pages of Cooke's book, the two reconciled amicably and *The Principles of Scientific Management* was published in 1910.

In an April 2017 article in the *PM World Journal*, Professor Darren Dalcher provides a detailed composition of Taylor's impact of applying scientific management to both task execution and management philosophy. It's in Dalcher's description of Taylor's idea of "separating thinking from doing" that exemplifies the foundations of project management philosophy as "the principle of separating the planning and design from execution, and the intended desire of freeing the workers from the need to think, flow naturally from the desire to simplify tasks, improve efficiency and throughput, reduce waste and increase monitoring and control." (Darren Dalcher 2017). These principles are the bedrock of project management before project management was a recognized profession.

The impact Frederick W. Taylor had on industrialization, management philosophy, and project management cannot be overstated. He was able to influence global practices in manufacturing, management philosophy, and project management. As a testament to his lasting impact, in 2011, the *Journal of Business Management* published an entire issue dedicated to Frederick W. Taylor, with the first article titled, "Frederick

Winslow Taylor: Reflections on the Relevance of the Principles of Scientific Management 100 Years Later" (Giannantonio 2011).

Principles of Scientific Management Pioneers Abroad

While Frederick W. Taylor was making a name for himself as a pioneer of scientific management in the West, there were contemporaries in the east that had, in their own right, made revolutionary contributions to the field of scientific management as well. Possibly none more well-known than Henri Fayol (1841–1925) and to a much lesser extent, Karol Adamiecki (1866–1933).

Fayol, a Frenchman born in Istanbul, Ottoman Empire, was a civil engineering of mines by trade and well known for his scientific knowledge of coal. He was familiar with the work of Taylor and developed his own administrative model that was based on, "a positivist methodology, which focused on observing the facts, making experiences, and extracting rules" (History-biography 2019). Fayol elevated to the position of CEO of Compagnie Commentary Fourchambault et Decazeville, having rescued the company from financial ruins. During his illustrious career, Fayol was an accomplished author, speaker, and businessman, well known for his many theories of business management, the "14 Principles of Management" was among the most notable, and has been credited as being the "real father of modern management" (Kukreja n.d.).

Karol Adamiecki (1866–1933) was a lesser known but earlier adopter of scientific management. He developed in Poland the "harmonogram" in 1896, at its core, used strips of paper to illustrate how long it took for each step in an operational processes to complete before the next step could begin. The simple illustration showing time and dependency from one step to the next made it easy to highlight bottlenecks in a process that could be addressed quickly. Using the model to identify production issues in a steel mill he worked in helped increase output by 100 percent in one year. The model created a stir in 1903 after it was presented to the Society of Russian engineers, making Adamiecki the leading authority of management in Poland. The harmonograph was reviewed by a disciple of Frederick W. Taylor, Henry L. Gantt, who made a few changes to Adamiecki's model and called it his own.

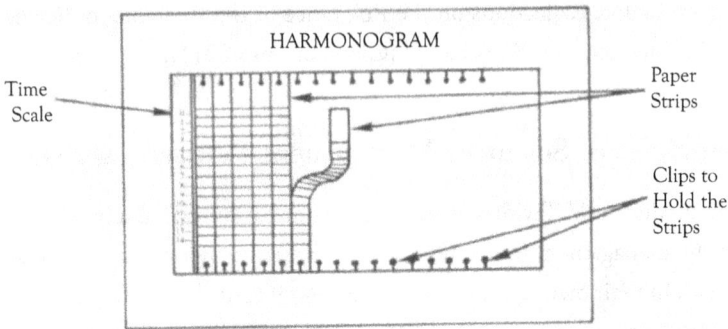

Adamiecki's "harmonogram." aom.org

The Gantt Chart

Henry L. Gantt (1861–1919) graduated from Johns Hopkins College in 1880 and soon after qualified as a mechanical engineer. From 1887 to 1893, he worked at Midvale Steel Company in Philadelphia, where he became assistant to the Chief Engineer at the time, Frederick W. Taylor. Having worked closely together for years, Gantt was a devout follower of Taylor, also using principles of scientific management to gain production efficiencies. It was Gantt's philosophy that "it was only the application of scientific analysis to every aspect of work which could produce industrial efficiency, and that improvements in management came from eliminating chance and accidents" (Peterson 1987).

While Gantt made numerous contributions to the application of scientific principles, his most noteworthy was what is known by his namesake, the "Gantt chart" (Figure 1.1) Inspired by the war efforts of 1917, the Gantt chart first started as an illustration of productivity of a person, machine, and so on. by putting a list of names on the *Y*-axis of the chart and productivity milestones along the *X*-axis; if the desired productivity level was reached, a square was shaded in black, and if not, in red. Gantt later revised his chart not to show productivity any longer but on time. The end result was a bar chart that showed how work was completed over time until it was complete. The Gantt continues to be used to this day having gone through several enhancement iterations along the way.

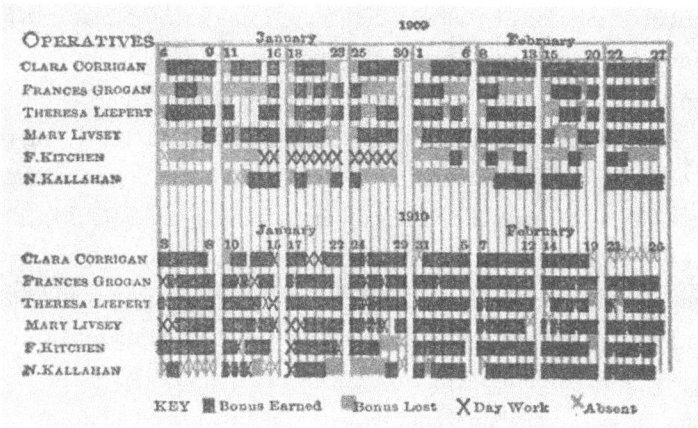

Figure 1.1a Original Gantt chart

Source: Gantt (1919).

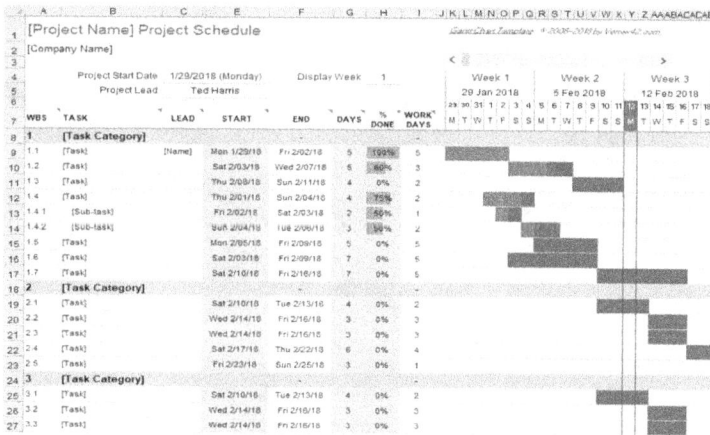

Figure 1.1b Modern Gantt chart

Source: Wittwer (2019).

The 20th Century and Beyond

The world witnessed unprecedented changes in the twentieth century, including two world wars, two industrial revolutions, an estimated growth in world population from 1.6 to 2.2 billion people, and the emergence of new technologies impacting every aspect of life. In order to successfully navigate the turbulent waters of change, the need for structured, innovative solutions to solve increasingly complex problems was paramount. As a result, advancements in engineering projects, business management, and project management accelerated accordingly.

Two notable developments in project management scheduling techniques during that time was the creation of both the project evaluation and review technique (PERT) and critical path method (CPM). PERT uses shapes like squares or circles to represent tasks or milestones that are connected by lines (or vectors), which illustrate the sequence and dependencies that exist between tasks arriving at a total duration for a specified project. The PERT model was originally created in 1957 by the United States Navy to facilitate complicated military projects but has been adopted by numerous industries worldwide. Figure 1.2 is an example of a PERT model.

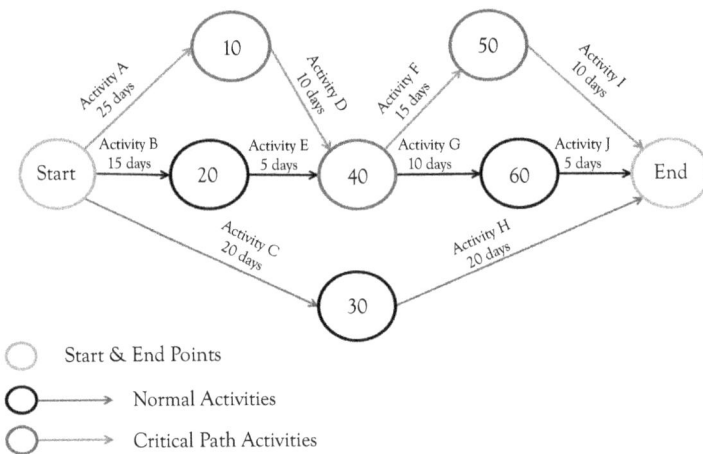

Figure 1.2 PERT model

Source: Shuttleworth (2017).

The CPM model was also created in the late 1950s by James Kelley of Remington Rand and Morgan Walker of Dupont. Its purpose was to manage the activities of a project to control cost and time. Its objective differed from that of the PERT model as the PERT model's purpose was to manage the uncertain task of a project to control time. Figure 1.3 is an example of a CPM model.

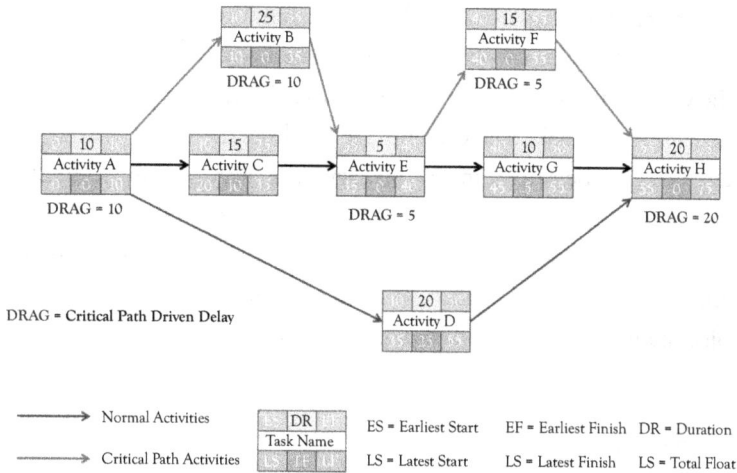

Figure 1.3 CPM model

Source: Shuttleworth (2017).

The space race of the late 1950s and the 1960s sparked an interest in project management beyond that of World War I, engineering marvels such as the Empire State Building (1931) and Golden Gate Bridge (1937), and World War II. In 1969, two colleagues—Jim Snyder of Smith, Kline and French Laboratories and Dr. J. Gordon Davis of Georgia Tech—discussed project management over dinner and felt that project managers from all industries should have a place to meet and share ideas. The discussions led to the advent of the Project Management Institute (PMI), founded by Snyder, Gordon, Eric Jenett, E. A. "Ned" Engman, and Susan Gallagher. In 1984, PMI launched its first Project Management Professional (PMP) certification, which has since become in industry gold standard in project management expertise. By the 1990s, the PMI had over 90,000 members and by 2020 reported over 600,000 members in its 2019 Annual Report.

As projects grow in risk and complexity due to lightning speed developments in technology, the twenty-first century must continue to make advancements in project management to solve the world's ever-evolving problems. While advancements have been made in various areas of project management including developments in project management approaches such as waterfall and Agile techniques, project management tools such as Microsoft Project, JIRA, and Hive, collaborative tools such as Skype, Zoom, and WebEx, as well as highly specialized certifications such as Agile Certified Practitioner, Certified Scrum Master, and Master Project Manager, additional advancements are needed. The project manager of today needs to be skilled in risk management, negotiations, technology, human resources, organizational behavior, and communications to name a few. The only way to build these skills is by advocating for and participating in the meeting, collaborating, training, and sharing of ideas so the project manager can succeed professionally and personally.

CHAPTER 2

Step-by-Step Project Management for U.S. Bankers

Project management is not an equation but an artform that, when executed properly, will increase the project's probability for success. Success in this context refers to a completed project, on time, and within the original project budget. In order to achieve project management success consistently, the project manager must follow a project management process that is simple, repeatable, and effective. This chapter gives a look at the steps to follow for a sound project management process and will then expand on each step to complete a comprehensive framework bank project managers should follow to increase the probability of success for bank projects of any size or complexity.

The Steps

Step 1: Approve the Project	Step 6: Business Requirements
Step 2: Project Stakeholders	Step 7: Technical/Functional Requirements
Step 3: Project Charter	Step 8: Product Development & System Testing
Step 4: Project Plan	Step 9: User Acceptance Testing (UAT)
Step 5: Associated Plans	Step 10: Implement the Solution & Close the Project

Step One: Approve the Project

The first step in any bank project management process is to gain approval for a project. Most banks will follow a process of surveying all the business lines within the bank determining what its project needs are and rank those projects by low, medium, and high criticality. Once all businesses have completed the survey, the complete list of projects is reviewed by an executive committee that will award or deny project proposals. The approved projects will be assigned to the requisite business lines and the process of forming a project team begins. The project approval process will be different in small, medium, large, and mega-banks as smaller institutions may have limited project management staff whereas large and mega-banks may have dedicated project management offices with teams of project managers. Regardless of the size of the institution, the project approval process should always be the first step in the project management process.

Step Two: Project Stakeholders

Once the project has been formalized, received financing, and has been assigned a project manager, the project manager should then meet with the project sponsor in person. If an in-person meeting is not possible, a dedicated video call or telephone call is the next best option. A project manager should never introduce himself or herself to the project sponsor via blind email as that will not only look poorly upon the project manager, but he or she will also lose credibility with the project sponsor.

During the meeting with the project sponsor, the project manager should gain a high-level understanding of the project and potential requirements, an idea of what business groups will be needed on the project team be it technology, legal, vendor management, compliance, or operations, and what the project sponsor's expectations are regarding project roles and responsibilities, project timeline, and communication preferences.

After meeting with the project sponsor, the project manager should begin forming the project team by contacting the businesses recommended by the project sponsor. The other businesses should assign a representative who will be a project stakeholder responsible for attending (or delegating) project meetings, reviewing and signing off on project documents, and approve the final product. Once all business lines have representation on the project, the core project team should be firmly established.

Step Three: Project Charter

When creating project management documents, there is no prescribed format for documents such as the project charter, project plan, business requirements, or testing documents. However, it is advantageous for each institution to create standardized project management templates that can be used repeatedly for any project. Standardized documentation provides consistency to the project management process, which in turn, reduces the likelihood of project discourse as project team members and stakeholders are familiar with standardized documents and processes. For the purposes of this chapter, it is presumed there is no prescribed format for project documents but will address elements to be included for each.

Once the project management team has been identified, the project manager should draft the project charter. In any project management process, the project charter is the most important document and should include identification of all project team members and stakeholders with associated roles and responsibilities, the business need/opportunity that exists to undertake the project, the business case highlighting the expected benefits of the project, the project scope, the project risks, issues, dependencies and constraints, the project assumptions, the project high-level business requirements, the project milestones with tentative completion dates, and a designated space where the project sponsor will sign off with approval and the date of approval.

It is important to note that the initial project charter draft will go through several iterations of edits until final approval is given. As such, each time the charter is edited, a "version history" section within the charter should capture the charter author, anyone who edited the document, when, and the updated version number. Each version should be saved separately, or at a minimum, track changes on all edits until final approval is given. Once the final approval is given, any changes to the charter should be proposed to the project stakeholders, reviewed, and approved.

Any approved changes should be updated in a new version of the project charter and circulated to the project team for reference.

What makes the project charter the most important document is that once approved, the charter becomes the foundation for the entire project. It recognizes the project manager, the project sponsor, the project objectives, the project requirements, and the project timeline. The charter will be the one document that every project team member will turn to when there are disagreements about what should or should not be included as part of the project, as well as reinforcement of the project goals and expected outcome. No other project document carries that kind of influence and authority.

Step Four: Project Plan

After obtaining approval on the project charter, the bank project manager should then draft the project plan. The project plan should include a list of major and minor milestones with associated deliverable dates. At a minimum, the project plan should include business requirement completion dates, any technological development dates, system testing dates, user acceptance test dates, and most importantly, an implementation or "go-live" date. The implementation date is when the project should be turned on and the business should start reaping the benefits originally identified to justify the project's undertaking.

Unlike the project charter, the project plan is more fluid. Even the best laid project plans will change due to either foreseen or unforeseen circumstances and the project plan will incorporate those changes accordingly. Additionally, because of its fluidity, it is not typical for the project plan to go through the formal approval process every time there is an update. It is up to the project manager to make the necessary changes and communicate the updates to the project team.

One important note to keep in mind when updating the project plan is that some milestones are either partially or completely dependent on other milestones to start or finish before the next milestone can start or finish. These dependencies need to be fully understood and updated appropriately as changes to the plan occur. The project manager is responsible for understanding these dependencies and making adjustments accordingly.

Step Five: Associated "Plans"

Once the project plan is in place, many project management frameworks or processes recommend adding other "plans" to the project such as a communications plan, risk management plan, and human resources plan. This approach is completely acceptable but not realistic in bank project management. The typical "plans" are usually communication plans, risk management plans, and change control plans. Communication plans and change control plans detail what the project communication approach is and what the change control process is but those plans will remain static and do not change. Therefore, these items can be addressed in documents like the project charter and do not require a stand-alone plan on its own.

The risk management plan is not static and will change through the course of the project, particularly during the business requirement gathering and technological development phases when the probability of breakdowns is highest. The risk management plan is basically a repository of what risks and issues are present, the owner of each risk and issue, and updates to the risk or issue with anticipated completion dates. It is important to note that the cost associated with risks and issues goes up as the project matures since changes are easier to make at the beginning of a project than at the end of a project. As such, it is important that risks and issues are identified and remediated as early in the process as possible.

Step Six: Business Requirements

With all plans in place, the next step in the banking project management process is to write the business requirements. It is unusual that a project manager would have enough subject matter expertise to independently write business requirements so the project manager will have to schedule a series of meetings with project stakeholders to ensure the business requirements are comprehensive.

The business requirements should include the list of stakeholders, a summary of the project goals and expectations, what is in and out of scope, known risks, issues, dependencies, and constraints, assumptions about the project requirements that should be satisfied (more on this in a moment), and an in-depth, highly detailed requirements section that provides as much detail as possible about each requirement. Assumptions about business requirements may include statements such as the following:

- The development team will publish technical specifications as needed.
- Any change control requests must be approved prior to technical development updates.
- System response times should not exceed maximum limit expectations.

With regard to the detailed requirements section, it is always a good idea to create a numbering convention for the business requirements so that each requirement can be matrixed to a functional specification, business test, and outcome to ensure each requirement is tested and accounted for. For example, let's say you have three requirements, 1A, 1B, and 1C and requirement 1A is aligned to functional specification 15. Assuming test for requirement 1A is successful, the testing matrix may look something like this:

Requirement	Functional Spec	Date Tested	Successful (Y/N)	Comments
1A	15	Jan. 1, 2020	Y	N/A

The matrix provides an easy and reliable memorialization of requirements, associated functional specification, and testing outcome information that is simple to follow and well understood by people both inside and outside of the project team.

The business requirements should be reviewed and approved by all stakeholders. Once the requirements are approved, any changes to the requirements should first be reviewed and approved by the project sponsor and then circulated to project stakeholders for reference. If a change in business requirements impact the project timeline and/or project budget, a more detailed explanation of the impact should be provided to the project sponsor so he or she can make an informed decision as to whether to proceed with the proposed change or not.

Step Seven: Technical/Functional Specifications

The next step in the banking project management process is for the development team to write both the technical and functional specification documents. The project manager should schedule a series of meetings with the development team to review the business requirement document in depth so there is a clear understanding of the development expectations. Once the development team is comfortable with the development expectations, they can then draft the technical specification document first and then the functional specification document. One important note about the technical specification document is that it should be written in layman terms that can be understood by nontechnical people even though the core components will be technical in nature.

The functional specifications document should be a blueprint for business people how the developed product will work. For example, if requirement 1A is for a user to gain access to a software program by entering in his ID and password, then the functional specification document should say something like,

Requirement 1A: User Should Gain Access to Software Application
In order to gain access to the software application, the user will type the URL into the Web browser, arrive at the landing page, enter their ID in the ID Number field, enter their password in the Password field, hit enter, and then have access to the software application.

While the technical specification and functional specification documents are being drafted, the project manager's only responsibility during this time is to ensure that both documents are comprehensive, completed on time, circulated for approval by all stakeholders, and ultimately approved by all stakeholders. Just as with other project documents, there could be several iterations of the technical and functional specification documents until all stakeholders are in agreement with the document contents.

Step Eight: Product Development and Systems Testing

After the technical and functional specification documents are approved, the development team should now develop the actual solution. The bank project manager should hold regular project meetings to get updates from the development team to make sure there are no new risks or issues as a result of development efforts and that the development team remains on schedule for testing and deployment.

Once the development team has completed its development, they must test the product in a testing environment to make sure it meets the business requirements, performance standards, and does not contain any known development bugs. System test results should be shared with the project manager and broader project team to maintain good communication and project continuity. Any bugs found during system testing are required to be fixed prior to handing the product off for the business team to test.

Step Nine: User Acceptance Testing (UAT)

While the development team was doing the actual development of the product, the project manager should be drafting UAT test scripts. There should be at least two types of UAT test scripts drafted by the project manager: UAT test scripts that are a straightforward, step-by-step process a user would follow to ensure that each requirement achieves the expected outcome, similar to the functional specification document, and "Red Team" testing where the project manager drafts test scripts that are purposefully trying to trigger error messages and other anomalies that the average user may experience.

Depending on the situation, there may be a need for regression testing in addition to straightforward and red team testing. Regression testing is used when there are multiple phases to a project and testing is conducted on the most recent installment and all previous installments to ensure the new installment did not disrupt the previous installments. For example, if there are three phases to a project, phase 1 will be tested independently, phase 2 will be tested independently and a retest (or regression test) of phase 1 will be conducted, and phase 3 will be tested independently, along with a retest of phases 1 and 2.

Using the example of requirement 1A, mentioned previously, a straightforward UAT test script may look something like this:

Requirement	Test Step	Expected Outcome	Successful (Y/N)
1A	User enters URL into Web browser	User is successfully taken to website	Y
	User enters ID into ID field	User is able to enter a series of numbers, letters, and characters into ID field	Y
	User enters password into password field and presses enter	User is able to enter a series of numbers, letters, and characters into password field, presses enter, and is taken to the software application	Y

Similarly, a "Red Team" test script may look something like this:

Requirement	Test Step	Expected Outcome	Successful (Y/N)
1A	User enters URL into Web browser	User is successfully taken to website	Y
	User enters non-numeric characters into the numeric only ID field	The user receives an error message that says, "Numeric values only"	N—the user was able to enter non-numeric characters as an ID and the field should be limited to numeric values only

It is the project manager's responsibility to ensure that each requirement is captured in a test script, that the Red Team test scripts are comprehensive, and that the expected outcomes for each test are successful. In the Red Team example above, this item would be labeled as a "bug" or "defect" and reported to the development team to fix (the development team will specify their preference for reporting bugs/defects during the UAT phase). Once all requirements are tested and there are no outstanding bugs, the business should sign off on UAT, paving the way for the product to be implemented.

Step 10: Implement the Solution and Close the Project

Once UAT is complete and the project sponsor has signed off on the testing outcomes, the development should be greenlighted to move the finished product from the test environment and into production. This is typically and intentionally done after hours on Friday or over the weekend to ensure that moving a new program into production does not interfere with daily operations or systems. It gives the development team time to implement the product and run some test scenarios outside of peak business hours to ensure it is working properly. The business team is called in early on Monday to test the final product in development once again to ensure that it is working properly and there are no disruptions to existing processes. Presuming all goes well over the weekend and Monday morning, both the project manager and business team will be monitoring performance for a specified period of time, usually two weeks to ensure there are no bugs or defects.

The last step in the banking project manager's process is to properly close the project. This requires gathering and organizing all project documents, meeting notes, testing outcomes, project plans, budgets, legal documents, and anything else that was associated with the project into a single package. It is the project manager's responsibility to include a project summary of the entire process including what worked, what did not work, how obstacles were overcome, what solutions were used, and how all of these factors influenced the overall project. This component of the project management process is critical for several reasons, the two most important are that having all of this information packaged properly allows for future review of the project process from internal audit or bank regulators, and that it provides a historical view on how the project was managed so that future projects that are similar in nature could use a "best practices" referential.

Conclusion

As stated in the very first sentence of this chapter, project management is not an equation but an artform. Being that project management is an artform, it leaves room for flexibility and creativity, but more importantly requires expert judgment, communication, and organization. Having a project management process that is designed to maximize these factors highly increases the project's probability for success. As such, the project management process described in this chapter is standard for most U.S. banks and is used over and over to achieve the highest levels of success possible.

CHAPTER 3

Introduction to Agile Project Management in Banking

Prior to 2001, bank project management consisted of "handshake" agreements between the sponsoring business group and the technology group, both agreeing to a set of business requirements, technological development, and deliverable timeframe. That was about it. There was no project charter, risk plan, communication plan, or any other type of project governance or administration. That is not to say project frameworks and tools did not exist as they most certainly did; it was just that American banks largely had not embraced them. The project management process loosely followed a "waterfall" approach and "Agile" was nothing more than a word in the dictionary.

This chapter will focus on first introducing the Waterfall project management process, its advantages and disadvantages, and when best to use it. The following sections will look at the Manifesto for Agile Software Development, the Agile development process, the different types of Agile development methodologies, the advantages and disadvantages of using Agile development, and how it is used in U.S. banks today.

Waterfall Project Management Process

The Waterfall project management process is an old and traditional way of managing bank projects. It is linear in nature where one project management phase must be completed and signed off on by all parties before the next phase can begin. Each proceeding phase is 100 percent dependent on the preceding phase to be completed before it can begin. Therefore, if there are five phases to your project and you decide during phase three you want to make a change, all previous phases will be impacted by that decision.

There are five phases to the Waterfall project management methodology: requirements, design, implementation, verification, and maintenance. Some practitioners acknowledge two additional components at the beginning of the Waterfall process, conception and initiation, which includes the project idea and baseline (conception) and definition of scope, purpose, and deliverables (initiation) (smartsheet 2020), but either are acceptable as there is no material change in the project management process itself.

A definition of each Waterfall project management phase is as follows:

- Requirements: all requirements are defined and documented at the beginning of the project; these documents become the baseline for the overall project.
- Design: ideas are brainstormed, agreed upon, and development work begins; all design documents must be reviewed, approved, and signed off on before moving to the implementation phase.
- Implementation: all development work is implemented at the same time; think of it as simply flipping the project work switch to "on."
- Verification: testing the end-result to ensure project objectives are met and everything is working as it should, which includes both functionality and performance testing (an example of functionality is that if the program is to transfer money from one place to another, the program actually does that; an example of performance means that if you click on something, the program is designed to respond in two seconds or less and a response above 2 seconds would be considered a defect).
- Maintenance: ongoing system support is provided to ensure project stability and updates are made to ensure the ongoing viability of the program.

It is because of the linear nature and dependency of the waterfall project management process that lends itself to the name, "Waterfall" because a visualization of each process follows a waterfall type of trajectory (Figure 3.1).

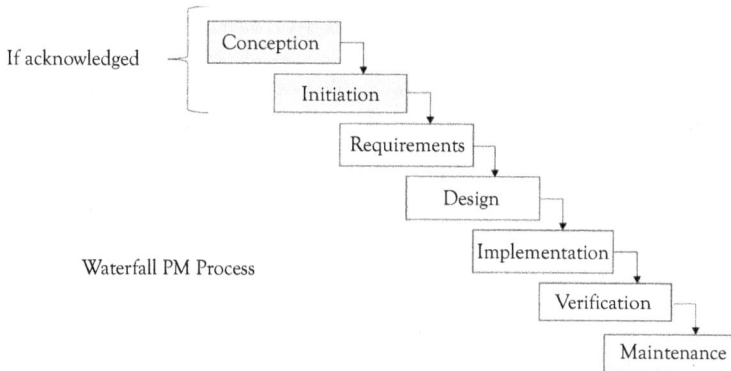

Figure 3.1 Waterfall project management process

The advantages of using a Waterfall model are that the steps are sequential; one cannot begin before the other one completes, analysis can be done at each phase to ensure there are no major risks or issues, and testing is done at the very end to ensure all objectives of the project have been met. The disadvantages of using a Waterfall model are that the end client is largely removed from the process and the difficulty to make changes at any point in the process, neither of which are popular within banking as there is a need for flexibility and fluidity versus rigidity.

The Waterfall methodology works best for small projects which is why it was loosely used in the U.S. banking industry prior to 2001. There was no need for major technological advancements due to two major contributing factors. One was the lack of technological solutions for archaic banking platforms which forced banks to make only small to moderate changes in its capabilities and two, the unwillingness of the bank customer to embrace new banking technology. Customers still wanted to walk into a bank to conduct basic banking transactions such as cashing or depositing a check, withdrawing money, or opening a savings account. It was not until these dynamics changed that opportunities to boost technological capabilities presented themselves, requiring a less rigid, more scalable, more fluid project management process.

Manifesto for Agile Software Development

The Agile project management methodology was born out of software development companies of the 1990s who experienced a high rate of project failures and lengthy project management completion timelines that were looking for, and in desperate need of "lightweight" project management solutions. Several new project management processes were developed but in 2001, 17 software developers met in Snowbird, Utah to discuss, create, and sign what has become known as the "Manifesto for Agile Software Development."

The Manifesto for Agile Software Development contained four key values and 12 development principles. The four key values are:

1. Individuals and interactions over processes and tools
2. Working software over comprehensive documentation
3. Customer collaboration over contract negotiation
4. Responding to change over following a plan (Eby 2016)

The 12 development principles are:

1. Customer satisfaction through early and continuous software delivery
2. Accommodate changing requirements throughout the development process
3. Frequent delivery of working software
4. Collaboration between the business stakeholders and developers throughout the project
5. Support, trust, and motivate the people involved
6. Enable face-to-face interactions
7. Working software is the primary measure of progress
8. Agile processes to support a consistent development pace
9. Attention to technical detail and design enhances agility
10. Simplicity
11. Self-organizing teams encourage great architectures, requirements, and designs
12. Regular reflections on how to become more effective (Eby 2016)

Agile Project Management Process

Having referenced the Manifesto for Agile Software Development's key values and development principles, it is important to understand what exactly an Agile project management process is. A comprehensive definition is provided by John Paul Mueller in a 2007 article for CIO stating, "Agile programming breaks down an application development project into small modularized pieces. Each piece, addressed one at a time, in a very short time frame, adds to the application and represents a complete part of the functionality. You can deploy the partial application and expect people to accomplish some level of work with it, even if the application doesn't do everything you intend it to do in the long run." (Mueller 2007)

As you can see in Mueller's explanation, an Agile project management approach is any project management approach that breaks a project down into smaller components and addresses each component as a mini-project until the overall project is complete. Figure 3.2 is a basic workflow that illustrates one way how an Agile project management process works.

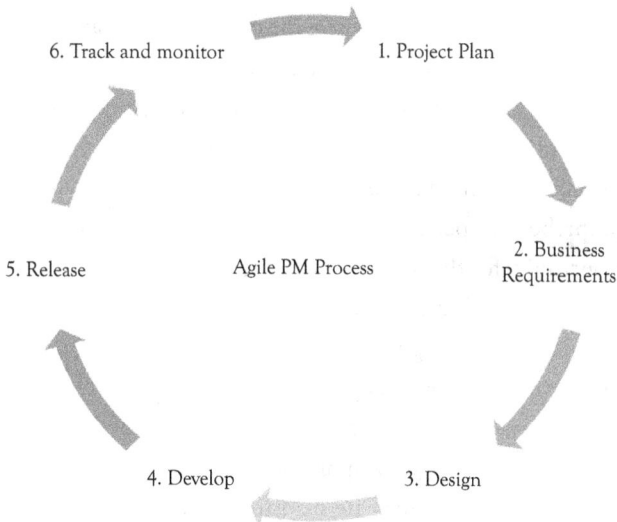

6. Track and monitor   1. Project Plan

5. Release   Agile PM Process   2. Business Requirements

4. Develop   3. Design

Figure 3.2 Agile project management process

1. *Project Plan*: The project manager meets with the business to hear what the project idea is, expectations for functionality, and the

business goals the business wants to achieve as a result of the project. The project manager then writes up a proposal to the development team to review inclusive of high level requirements, assumptions, and what is in and out of scope. The development team will then review the project proposal and map out a blueprint of project "sprints," a breakdown of the project into individual components that can be developed independently of each other, to illustrate how the project will be completed. Think of a puzzle where the pieces are sprints and the completed puzzle is the project.

2. *Requirements phase*: For illustration purposes only, let's presume the development team identified four sprints are needed to complete the project. The business would then identify, document, and submit only the first sprint's business requirements to the development team to begin work. Business requirements for the additional sprints are not considered at this point in the project and will not be considered until sprint 1 is at or near completion. The development team will let the project manager know which sprint will be developed next and when to start collecting business requirements.

3. *Design*: This is the period where the development team creates mock-ups of the first sprint's proposed solution, possibly including work-flows and other visualizations on what the sprint result will look and feel like. Depending on the sprint itself, the development team may also present demos of the first sprint solution to provide a more comprehensive perspective of how development is going. This is an opportunity for the business to review progress and make suggestions on how to tweak the solution to better align with their expectations. Once the sprint design is agreeable to the business, both parties agree and move to the sprint development phase.

4. *Development phase*: The development team "codes" or "builds" the solution that was agreed upon for the first sprint during the design phase. Regular meetings are held to further clarify the first sprint's final product, highlighting any risks or issues that arise and creating a mitigation plan to solve for those risks or issues. When development has progressed far enough, the development team will contact the project manager to start collecting business requirements for sprint two's development.

5. *Release*: During the release phase, the developed solution is moved to a "test" environment that simulates what happens in production (production is the live environment where all day to day business and processes take place) so members of the business team can test the product to ensure there are no bugs in the product, it works as it is intended, and all expected outcomes are achieved without issue. Once all tests are complete and the business signs off on the final product, the first sprint solution is moved to the production environment.

6. *Track and monitor*: The first sprint solution may now be used by the business since it is an independent component for the overall project. If the business decides to use the solution for sprint one, they can check the stability of the solution, its functionality, and identify issues that may have not been identified during the testing phase.

This version of an Agile project management process could work for small- to large-scale projects. For a smaller project, there may only be one sprint needed to complete the whole project. For larger projects, the project may be broken into many sprints, as many that would be needed to complete the whole project. Regardless of the number of sprints, the project manager would follow the same trajectory for each sprint, working on a plan, gathering requirements, allowing for the design and development to take place, testing and releasing that sprint's solution, and finally, monitoring how that sprint functions in production.

Different Types of Agile Development Methodologies

According to Blueprint, an enterprise automation expert, the most widely used Agile methodologies include: Agile Scrum Methodology, Lean Methodology, Kanban, Extreme Programming (XP), Crystal, Dynamic Systems Development Method (DSDM), and Feature Driven Development (FDD) (Blueprint Agile Methodologies 2020). Following is a brief description on each:

- *Agile Scrum methodology* is an incremental approach to software development run in sprints of two to four weeks;

it develops the most important features first to deliver a superior product.

- *Lean methodology* was developed by a Japanese engineer, Taiichi Ohno, in the 1950s and 1960s. Lean methodology refers to manufacturing and is concerned about production process efficiency versus a development process.

- *Kanban development* is similar to Lean methodology but applies its methods to improve work across human systems by identifying bottlenecks and applying resources to those efforts.

- *Extreme programming* uses short development cycles to improve software quality and focuses on the "extreme" components required to add the most value, tuning everything else out.

- *Crystal* is a software development approach that focuses on people and their interactions more than on a process or framework; the belief is that how people interact have the biggest impact on a project so let them figure out what's the best way to work on a project.

- *DSDM* is the framework consists of four phases that address the entire project lifecycle and impact on the business: feasibility and business study, functional model/prototype iteration, design and build, and implementation.

- *FDD methodology* "is customer centric, iterative, and incremental, with the goal of delivering tangible software results often and efficiently"; status reporting is provided at all levels to help track progress.

Based on different types of Agile methodologies, it is important to understand the nature of the project itself before choosing which methodology works best for your situation. The next section will highlight the advantages and disadvantages of using an Agile methodology which may help you decide.

Advantages and Disadvantages of Using Agile Methodology

While there are many advantages and disadvantages of using Agile methodology, this section will review five advantages and five disadvantages of using it from a U.S. bank setting.

Five Advantages

- *Faster deployment*: Because each component of the software is developed independent of each other, as soon as one component is complete, it can be put into production ready for use; this is incredibly important in banking especially if the project is regulatory in nature, geared toward increasing revenue or decreasing costs. It also eliminates the potential for scope creep, or extending the scope beyond what the individual project phase was drafted for completion.

- *Less paperwork*: Agile is not meant to be overly administrative, as such, people can focus on those tasks that require the most attention without having to spend inordinate amounts of time pushing paper around.

- *Change management*: The ability to make changes in an Agile process is much easier and cheaper than in other processes, again because components are developed independently of each other.

- *Risk and issue management*: This process is much easier to execute because of the independent nature of each Agile component; as such, risks and issues can be addressed quicker mitigating the probability of a major disruption to the overall project.

- *Experimentation*: Developers have a lot of room to be creative and try different solutions for the project as they are not pigeon-holed into one solution or another; this is particularly helpful when developing complex projects where the final product is not entirely known when the project is started.

Five Disadvantages

- *Lack of documentation*: U.S. banks prefer that anything and everything gets documented, as such, an Agile methodology may be used however banks would continue to document progress regardless.
- *Inability to Measure Progress*: Banks need to be able to say with certainty when a project will be complete, what it will cost, and what business goals will be satisfied; because Agile develops components independently, it is not clear what type of progress is being made as progress happens across cycles and not all at once—this is a critical disadvantage when resources are tied up for years and no clear progress can be communicated to management.
- *Project timeline*: With Agile, there really is no clear end to a project even though the goals of an individual project phase may be reached; questions arise about building off of the completed project or upgrading components that were developed first, stretching the project beyond what was originally intended (high probability for scope creep).
- *Team Dynamics*: Because there is a lot of creativity used in Agile, it requires the developers and customer to meet and discuss possibilities together; this is especially time-consuming for the business owners as their primary job of running that business does not stop for project management purposes.
- *Development strategy*: There are times when Agile breaks a project into components but some of those components are too big and need to be broken down even further; this can get confusing as it is difficult to plan for and explain how each of the components are related and how they are being developed (another major thorn in the side for U.S. banks).

How Agile Is Used in U.S. Banks

As with any organization, if there is an idea for a project at a U.S. bank, the idea must go through a review and approval process for the project to be initiated as a formal project complete with funding and allocation of resources. Once this has taken place, if the project is estimated to take longer than six months, it is practically certain that any U.S. bank will use some type of Agile methodology to complete the project.

The application of Agile in U.S. banks though is different than how Agile is intended to work. As mentioned previously, there are a lot of uncertainties using Agile methodologies and that does not align with U.S. bank project management processes. Uncertainties around development timelines, overall project budget, project progress, and scope creep are characteristics about Agile methodology U.S. banks do not like. As such, a project manager is always assigned to these projects. That is in direct conflict with the Agile Manifesto and Agile principles; nowhere does it reference the use of a project manager. Instead, the Agile Manifesto specifies, "...individuals and interactions over processes and tools." U.S. banks are conservative in nature and want to make sure someone is in control of a project at all times, hence, a project manager will be assigned to the project regardless of using an Agile methodology.

With a project manager in place, the project manager will be the person that goes between the developers and the business, therefore having a certain amount of authority over the project that is also in direct contradiction to Agile methodology. The U.S. bank wants its business to run its businesses and hires (hopefully) highly competent project managers to be a voice on the project that will gather business requirements, keep track of progress, and involve the business only when needed. This allows the business to manage the business and the project manager to manage the project, doing exactly what each role in the bank is intended to do.

Lastly, Agile methodology does not require a lot of project paperwork or administration. However, many U.S. bank projects are regulatory in nature and require a significant amount of paperwork and administration. Again, the project manager will ensure every aspect of the project is properly documented and classified so that evidence of the project progress can be demonstrated to regulators with ease. Not having a project manager in place for regulatory, Agile projects puts the bank at risk unnecessarily.

Conclusion

The majority of projects in U.S. banks use some type of Agile methodology to complete the project but use the role of the project manager to
oversee project progress and administration. While this may be in direct
conflict with Agile methodology, it is a necessary component to managing
projects in U.S. banks due to the regulatory nature in which it operates.
Other project methodologies may be used for smaller projects or projects that have a duration less than six months, but Agile is the preferred
method of project delivery in U.S. banks today.

CHAPTER 4

Using Bank Compliance Software

The International Compliance Association (ICA) cites five key functions of a financial services compliance department:

1. Identify the risks an organization faces and advise on them (identification).
2. Design and implement controls to protect the organization from those risks (prevention).
3. Monitor and report on the effectiveness of those controls in the management of an organization's exposure to risks (monitoring and detection).
4. Resolve compliance difficulties as they occur (resolution).
5. Advise the business on rules and controls (advisory) (ICA International Compliance Association 2020).

In order to properly execute against these key functions, a compliance department requires people with specialized knowledge and skills related to compliance, sophisticated tools and processes to enhance the efficiency, safety, and scalability of an organization, and a sustainable business structure flexible enough to account for changes in regulation, technology, and the crimes that are committed. This chapter will focus on specific functions of a compliance program and the compliance software programs used to accomplish these tasks, as well as the importance of having a safe, reliable compliance program. The appendix will include a list of compliance software applications with pros and cons for each.

Know Your Customer (KYC) and Anti-Money Laundering (AML) Screening

Before looking at the tools used by bank compliance programs for KYC and AML, it is important to understand exactly what KYC and AML screening are. KYC is the process of not only identifying a client but also creating the "risk profile" of a client. This means that in addition to identifying a client, the bank must also determine suitability and risk tolerance for that client. Suitability means that the products and services the person wishes to purchase aligns with his/her background. Those products and services then should be representative of his/her appetite for risk. For example, if your grandmother wanted to invest in U.S. Treasury securities, that is appropriate for someone with her background—an older person, possibly on a fixed income, a low tolerance for risk, and the safety and stability of U.S. Treasuries as an investment choice. On the other hand, It would not be suitable for your grandmother to invest in cryptocurrencies where the risk is incredibly high, prices are volatile, and she could lose everything. On-boarding questions during the KYC process will provide a comprehensive identity and risk profile for your grandmother to prevent conflicts like this from arising.

AML screening is performed to identify, mitigate, and prevent money laundering activities. Money laundering is the process criminals undertake when attempting to make the proceeds from their criminal activities (activities such as drug trafficking or terrorist funding) look legitimate by disguising the true source of those funds. There are three stages of money laundering:

1. Placement: putting cash from criminal activities into the financial system
2. Layering: conducting multiple, complex transactions in an attempt to disguise the true source of funds
3. Integration: creating what appears to be legitimate legal sources of those funds

As the criminal world grows in size, scope, and sophistication with improvements in technology, the challenge every bank faces is how to stay ahead of the financial crime curve and that is dependent on the efficacy of the tools it utilizes.

KYC Software

Typically, you would not find stand-alone software for KYC and a separate software for AML. The software would be an integrated tool that does both but are separated out for discussion purposes only. The focus will first be on KYC software and then AML software.

The purpose of KYC software is to assist the firm with "onboarding" customers by validating their identity and creating a risk profile for those individuals or businesses. Typical KYC software will have a list of questions that must be completed before an account can be opened, questions such as name, address, phone number, social security number, previous names, previous addresses, types of assets and the source that generated those assets (income, dividends, business venture, etc.), if the person is an owner, director, or stakeholder in another company, if the person holds a political office of any kind, and questions about risk tolerance such as what types of investments are you comfortable with, how much volatility you are comfortable with, and if you are seeking high returns, stable returns, or preservation of capital. Answers to all these questions are entered into the KYC software program and if there are no immediate red flags, an account number is generated for the customer.

The creation of the account number does not mean much until the backend processes are complete as well. While the front-end process of onboarding a client may seem straightforward, how the full onboarding process works, particularly with the KYC software, is far more complex. Figure 4.1 depicts the basic flow of a KYC system.

How long it takes to complete the full end-to-end client onboarding process is entirely dependent on how quickly the potential client submits his or her paperwork. As such, the process can transpire over days or weeks. However, the work done by the KYC software is done quickly and efficiently in the nightly batch process.

Every financial firm has an "end-of-day" cutoff where no other business is accepted for that day and all that day's activities are "batched" together in various electronic files. The new account file, or KYC file, batches all

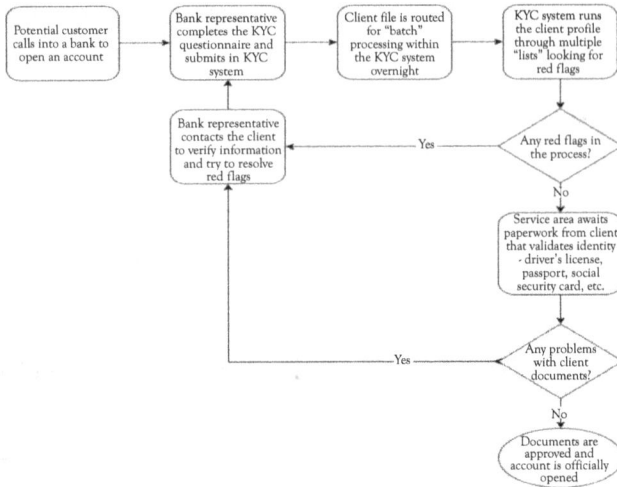

Figure 4.1 Basic KYC workflow

of the accounts that were entered into the KYC system throughout the day and runs the new account file through the KYC system once the file has been properly formatted and loaded for processing. The KYC system will then take all of the client data and run it against various "lists" to see if there are any red flags. Examples of the lists include, but is not limited to lists such as the Federal Bureau of Investigation (FBI) most wanted, Interpol most wanted, FinCEN, sanctions lists, and so on. If the client file does not trigger any red flags, the account along with the risk profile is pending approval.

If there are red flags generated during the KYC process, an electronic file of red flag profiles is sent to a service area who will then contact the potential customer to try and resolve whatever was causing a red flag. Red flags can be generated from something that was triggered when run against one of the mandated regulatory lists, the risk profile does not match the information the potential client provided, or possibly because the person submitted suspicious or incomplete identity validating paperwork. Regardless of why the red flag was triggered, the client service representative will work to resolve the problem, and if the problem cannot be resolved, the account is denied and a record of the denial is kept on file as part of an audit trail for the account opening process.

Some sophisticated banks can route red flags electronically, simplifying and expediting the follow-up process. This works by connecting service area representatives to the account opening platform. When red flags are identified overnight, they are sent electronically to a "central processing system" where bank representatives can work on the next item in the queue and update the information real time. As the representative input notes to the system, that information is memorialized for easy follow-up. For example, if an initial call goes out to a potential customer indicating the address on file does not match their paperwork, the representative can update the file with the outcome of the conversation. If the potential client calls back the next day and speaks to another representative, all of the notes from previous conversations are available to assist the client without delay. Having a streamlined process such as this makes it easier to monitor service customers, as well as report on the work being done and identify where bottlenecks exist.

The KYC process though is not just for new customers. When a customer is approved for an account, the risk profile of the client determines how often they will have to "recertify" their KYC credentials. The typical timeframe to recertify accounts is annually for high-risk, every two years for moderate risk, and every three years for low-risk customers.

AML Software

Most AML software is composed of a transaction monitoring component, a case management component, and an investigative platform component. The transaction monitoring component is highly complex as it looks at a multitude of factors to determine if the transaction is legitimate or not. Some factors include the dollar amount of each transaction, the volume of transactions (how many transactions are seen during a typical business day), if there are any suspicious features of the transaction such as the identity of the third party of a transaction or the origin and/or destination of the assets in the transaction, and how far the transaction strays from the client's risk profile. For example, if a client profile includes one deposit every week and a series of small transactions at grocery stores and gas stations, transactions that meet that criteria will not be flagged. However, if that client goes on a shopping spree two towns over and makes purchases in various stores, that could trigger a low-level red flag. Finally, if the client activity shows online purchases for expensive computer equipment originating across the country, that should be a significant red flag.

If something is anomalous for a transaction or transactions and a red flag is triggered, a notification is sent to a transaction monitoring area to begin investigating why the red flag was generated. The representative investigating the suspicious activity will utilize a case management system to log all information about the transaction as well as any additional notes that may exist at the time of the red flag. That representative will also utilize investigative tools to research the red flag, investigative tools such as negative news files, enhanced due diligence for politically exposed persons (PEPs), and so on. The representative is trying to determine if the transaction is legitimate or truly suspicious. Transactions that generate a red flag are oftentimes deemed as "false-positives," meaning the AML software flagged the activity as suspicious but upon investigation, it was determined to be legitimate. If, however, the investigation deems the activity to be truly suspicious, then there are multiple ways the situation could be handled but it usually requires documenting the information in the case management system *and* reporting the activity to the proper authorities.

Examples of a false-positive could be someone who deals in primarily low-dollar transactions all of a sudden deposits $50,000 in cash. Because the dollar threshold is much higher than a normal transaction for this client, it could be flagged as being suspicious. Upon investigation though, the person may have inherited money from a deceased loved one which legitimizes the transaction.

In an example of how a transaction or group of transactions would be suspicious is someone who's risk profile says that his only source of income is his salary as a mid-level compliance bank manager. However, the activity in his account shows a series of $9,999 deposits in cash each day for four days. Even though the transactions do not total the $10,000 currency transaction report requirement, this activity is well beyond that of a mid-level bank manager and should be investigated further.

Fraud Detection Software

In order for something to be considered fraud, two criteria must be met: the intent to deceive someone *and* the deception is meant to result in some kind of financial or personal gain. If the situation satisfies those two criteria, it can be considered fraud. Fraud can take on many forms in the banking industry and up until this point in time, fraud was usually in the form of something being stolen from someone, their identity, a credit/debit card number, checks, cash, or otherwise, and using that stolen item or items for personal gain. However, there is a new form of fraud called "synthetic fraud," which occurs when a fraudster combines stolen information, typically a social security number, with a fictitious name and driver's license to create an entirely new identity. That fraudster then uses the new identity to access products and services, particularly credit, to rack up charges he or she never intends to pay for.

While synthetic fraud may be relatively new in the financial services industry, in a 2019 article in *Forbes* titled, "Synthetic Identity Fraud Is the Fastest Growing Financial Crime—What Can Banks Do To Fight It?" Glen Larson cites that in a recent study by McKinsey, "...synthetic ID fraud is the fastest-growing type of financial crime in the U.S." and later cites that synthetic fraud costs lenders, "...more than $6 billion annually and the average loss at $10,000 per account" (Larson 2019).

In order to understand how synthetic fraud software works, one must first understand how the synthetic fraud process works. The United States is driven by a person's social security number to apply for any kind of financial services. Data breaches have exposed numerous social security numbers that are stolen and used to create fake identities. The fraudster will use that identity to apply for a loan or credit card and will be denied, but then eventually approved as the person builds up credit with the fake identity. Once a substantial credit level is reached, the person will "bust out" with large purchases, maxing out the credit and then simply disappear.

The software used to identify and capture synthetic fraud is a series of complicated algorithms that looks at every step of the customer lifecycle from onboarding through account transacting. However, the success of the software is dependent on having access to identify data breaches and comparing that information to new accounts so as to catch any wrongful identities before they have the ability to transact. As such, it is critical that synthetic identify software providers can work with global institutions that experience data breaches in order to program that information into their software and stay ahead of the financial crime curve.

In order for banks to better protect themselves against this type of fraud, they will need to employ tools capable of more sophisticated KYC investigations and introduce hard to replicate components of one's identity such as biometrics or facial recognition software.

Sanctions Software

In order to combat sanctions-related incidents, many banks have a financial crimes compliance area that investigates such activity. The people that work in this area are well trained in areas of sanctions and sanctions investigations, oftentimes incredibly knowledgeable in the regulations that govern sanctions and how to properly dissect transactions in the most granular of detail. They also rely on sophisticated software that supports sanctions investigations as well as supportive investigative platforms to conduct thorough research.

Sanctions software is focused on watchlist screening to compare clients and/or transactions against sanctions lists to ensure that either the bank's client or the bank client's client is not associated with known sanctions individuals or businesses. As transactions are occurring, the bank's transaction system is comparing those transactions to standard sanctions lists from the Office of Foreign Assets Control (OFAC), the European Union (EU), the United Nations, the World Bank, the specially designated nationals list, and many others. As the transactions are run against these lists, checks are done against both the transaction initiator and transaction beneficiary to ensure both parties are safe. This requires mountains of transactions and files to be run through sanctions screening systems to compare names, transaction directions, transaction sources, and transaction destinations to make sure that all parties in the transactions are approved.

In most domestic local, community, or regional banks, customer bases are relatively modest and transactions are oftentimes straightforward—basic lending, checking/ACH, credit/debit cards, and so on. However, for large, mega, and international banks that transact across borders, the transactions are much more complex. For example, an oil company in Saudi Arabia is going to ship 50 million gallons of crude oil to Brazil but needs financing for the trip as the counterparty will not pay for the oil until it is delivered. The Saudi Arabian oil company will approach an international bank for trade financing to make the trip agreeing to pay back the loan based on contractual stipulations. It is up to the bank to understand everything about the Saudi Arabian oil company, its owners, the Brazilian counterparty and everyone they do business with, along with every other customer the Saudi Arabian company does business with. The reason being is that sanctions compliance is intended to prevent transacting with any person or business prohibited by OFAC. If a transaction is deemed suspicious by the bank's sanctions screening software, the representative will then utilize investigative platforms to research all of this to determine if the transaction is safe or not.

Importance of a Compliance Program

Regardless of the size of the bank, the compliance department is critical to ensuring the safety and stability of the banking system and protecting the assets entrusted to them. The most well-known compliance regulations are KYC/AML and sanctions as those two areas of compliance cover a significant scope of banking regulations.

A comprehensive compliance program includes well trained staff, access to effective tools, the flexibility to adapt to a changing regulatory and technological environment, a strong communication network to share policies and procedures, review and administration of process controls, and a reporting platform capable of capturing and displaying current activities as well as trends over time.

As discussed in previous chapters, there are many regulators and regulations that govern the U.S. banking industry. The regulatory bodies that establish the regulations also govern the activities of each bank to ensure the safety and stability of the banking system, and do so by

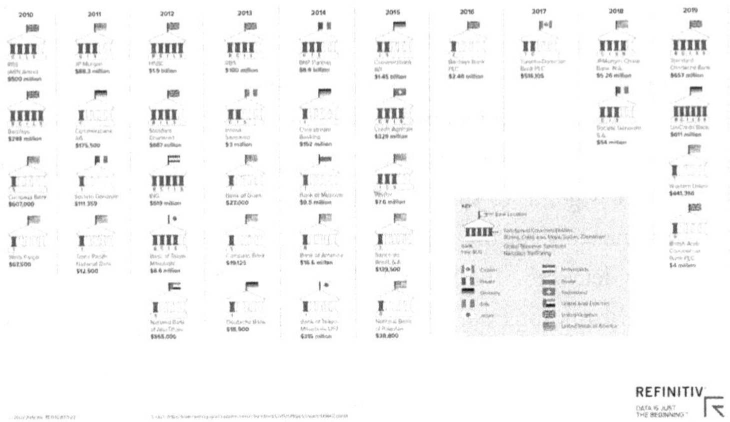

Figure 4.2 Fines for banks that breached U.S. OFAC sanctions

Source: Fines for Banks that Breached U.S. OFAC Sanctions 2020

conducting on-site investigations of banks and branches. Each bank must supply regulators with documentation that details the structure, underlying processes, and controls established by the compliance department to demonstrate adherence with banking regulations. Banks that either knowingly or unknowingly violate these regulations are fined, and at times, fined an exorbitant amount of money in reparation for the wrongdoing.

Figure 4.2 is a chart obtained from refinitiv.com illustrates the fines levied on banks from 2010 to 2019 for various sanctions violations. The chart provides the name of the bank, the banks' home country, the amount of the fine, and the sanctioned countries involved.

Appendix

Table 4.1 Comparison of AML software programs

	ACAMS Risk Assessment	Actimize	AML Risk Manager	Surety	SAS Anti-money Laundering
Starting Price	N/A	N/A	N/A	N/A	N/A
Best For	N/A	Cloud-based solution that helps businesses detect, prevent money laundering and fraud along with compliance violations	Offers specialized features for financial institutions, securities and investment firms, insurance companies, and corporate enterprises	N/A	Designed for banking and financial institutions that helps manage suspicious activity monitoring, reporting, alerts, and more
Ideal # of Users	N/A	N/A	2–1,000+	N/A	10–1,000+
Rating	★★★☆☆	★★★★☆	☆☆☆☆☆	★★★★☆	★★★★☆
Ease of Use	★★★★☆	★★★★★	☆☆☆☆☆	★★★★★	★★★★☆
Customer Support	★★★☆☆	★★★★★	☆☆☆☆☆	★★★★★	★★★★★
Features and Functionality	★★★☆☆	★★★★☆	☆☆☆☆☆	★★★★★	★★★★★
Value for Money	★★★☆☆	★★★★☆	☆☆☆☆☆	★★★★★	★★★★☆
Training	Not provided by vendor	Not provided by vendor	In person, live online, webinars, documentation	Not provided by vendor	Documentation

(AML Software 2020)

CHAPTER 5

Understanding Key Issues in Bank Project Management

During the first two decades of the twenty-first century, the United States has witnessed cataclysmic events such as the attacks on September 11, 2001, the second Gulf War, and most recently, the unprecedented COVID-19 pandemic that spread throughout not just the United States but the world. Over that same time-period, the United States has also witnessed several financial upheavals including the ".com" bubble burst of 2001, fallout from the September 11 attacks, and the CDO (collateralized debt obligation)/mortgage crisis of 2008 to name a few.

It is the job of the Federal Reserve and Federal Deposit Insurance Corporation (FDIC) to provide safety and stability to the U.S. banking industry as these events unfold. In so doing, new regulations are enacted, guidance is issued, and monetary policy is adjusted. The individual bank must adhere to the new regulations, adapt to the guidance issued, and provide essential banking services in response to monetary policy changes. While various areas of the bank must partner to implement the required changes, banks have embraced the use of project managers to execute these directives.

While project managers across all industries experience common challenges as it relates to the project management process, this chapter will review the key issues experienced by bank project managers with regards to the strategic, technological, budgetary, and political forces that influence bank project management, as well as the bank's organizational structure and the nature of the project itself be it regulatory, IT, new product offering, or policy related.

Strategic Issues

The first step in understanding strategic issues experienced by bank project managers, one must first define and agree on what a strategy is and why it is important. Ann Latham provides a comprehensive explanation in a 2017 article for *Forbes* magazine saying,

> A strategy is a framework for making decisions about how you will play the game of business. Without a strategic framework to guide these decisions, the organization will run in too many different directions, accomplish little, squander profits, and suffer enormous confusion and discord (Latham 2017).

Knowing that a strategy is a framework for making decisions to avoid confusion and discord, the first issue a bank project manager may encounter is what strategy should he/she use for managing his or her project. A Google search for "What is a good project management strategy" yields over 1.5 billion references while narrowing your search terms to "What is a good project management strategy for banking" drastically improves your chances for finding a good project management strategy citing only 391 million results (Google 2020). In other words, there are many opinions, articles, and recommendations for project management strategy, even as it relates to banking, but which strategy works?

U.S. banks are notorious for being stogey, old-fashioned institutions with stogey, old-fashioned philosophies. As such, a good project management strategy is one that is simple, easily repeatable, and fits with the culture and environment of the bank. The Project Management Institute provides one such strategy using a framework that includes five project management process groups and ten knowledge areas that, when used in conjunction with one another are simple and effective at managing projects. A project management process group is defined as, "A set of interrelated actions and activities performed to create a specified product, service, or result." (*A Guide to the Project Management Body of Knowledge* (*PMBOK Guide*) 5th edition 2013) and includes the Initiating Process Group, Planning Process Group, Executing Process Group, Monitoring and Controlling Process Group, and Closing Process Group. Each one of these process groups are used in every project and align with most U.S. banks' organizational culture.

A knowledge area is described as, "…a complete set of concepts, terms, and activities that make up a professional field, project management field, or area of specialization" (*A Guide to the Project Management Body of Knowledge* (*PMBOK Guide*) 5th edition 2013) and includes Project Integration Management, Scope Management, Time Management, Cost Management, Quality Management, Human Resource Management, Communications Management, Risk Management, Procurement Management, and Stakeholder Management. Unlike the project management processes that are used for each project, not all knowledge areas will be used for every project. It is at the discretion of the project manager which knowledge areas are essential to the project's success and should be aligned with the project management processes.

Technological Issues

For projects that require a technical solution, there are several main types of issues every project manager must contend with, specifically, identifying technological solutions best suited to address the business need, securing resources to develop and implement the desired technology, assisting with translating business requirements into technological solutions and forecasting how much implementing and using the technology costs.

When deciding which technological solution is best suited to address the business need, the project manager first needs to figure out if the technology can be developed "in-house," meaning bank-employed IT people will develop the solution, or if the project technology will be "off-the-shelf," meaning an external vendor will provide the solution. If the technology will be provided off-the-shelf, an "RFP" (request for proposal) should be issued to several vendors who can present a demonstration of its tools, capabilities, and costs to project stakeholders to help decide which solution best addresses the business need. While the project manager is instrumental in identifying options to solve the business problem, it is the project sponsor that will make the ultimate decision which solution to use.

Regardless of who develops the technological solution be it internal employees or external vendors, the project manager will then need to secure internal, bank IT employees to assist with implementing and deploying the solution. The internal IT team provides expertise with issues such as compatibility with existing bank infrastructure, security, and stability of the technology solution, calculating system response times if needed, and resource scheduling that will influence the overall project timeline. Securing IT resources in banks with a global presence often-times presents greater challenges as those resources could be located any-where in the world. As such, the project manager must deftly coordinate communications to ensure continuous development regardless of which time zone IT resources may be located in.

Once IT resources are in place, the project manager must work closely with someone in IT, most likely an IT project manager, to discuss the business requirements and expected results. Oftentimes, the project man-ager will not have, nor should have, the technical expertise of someone in IT, just as someone in IT should not have expert knowledge of how the business is run. It is the project manager's responsibility that the business requirements are then properly communicated to the IT team, the IT team has a clear picture of the requirements and expected results, and both teams agree to a project timeline and costs. If both business and IT resource are spread across the globe, there are time zone differences and potentially language barriers to overcome, so the project manager need to be aware of these dynamics and come up with the appropriate solution.

Budget Issues

Finally, and arguably, the most important issue faced by project managers is determining project costs. Determining project costs depends heavily on the style and approach the bank employs to their project budgets. Broadly speaking, project costs include the cost of internal IT people (usu-ally calculated in "man days" and equals the daily rate for one IT resource times the number of days to develop and implement the project), the cost for an off-the-shelf solution if needed, the cost to the external vendor to onboard the solution, and legal and/or administrative fees for contract preparation and review. Often times, the project manager's salary is not included in the project cost if the project manager is a full-time employee of the bank, but a project manager's salary may be included if the project manager is a consultant of the bank and not a full-time employee. Again, while the project manager will play an integral role in the project cost estimation process, the project sponsor has final approval on all estimated project costs before finalizing which solution best addresses the business need.

There are three main issues encountered when budgeting for project costs: securing funding for the project, ongoing budget maintenance (accounting for costs as they are incurred), and accounting for project budgets that extend to multiple fiscal periods.

Securing Funding

Securing funding for the proposed project is the most critical component of any project and project budget. Without funds aligned to a project, a project does not exist. The project manager must conduct high-level meetings with the business sponsoring the project, IT, legal, operations, finance, and others to discuss what business need exists and what solutions may be best to address that business need. Once an agreed upon solution is identified, IT teams will develop and present a service schedule with estimated development costs, legal will develop and present an estimation on legal and administrative costs, and operations will develop and present an estimation on training or processing costs. The project manager will aggregate all cost and submit for approval. Simultaneously, other project managers across the bank are doing the same thing to secure funding for his/her project so you end up with numerous projects competing for limited funding. Project committees comprised of high-level business, IT, finance, and legal review the project proposals and approve or reject in accordance with overall bank strategy and goals. If the project is approved, finance will allocate funding to the department to cover the project costs. Once the funding is received, the project manager starts the project management process having overcome the first major budgetary challenge.

Ongoing Budget Maintenance

The next budgetary issue a project manager will encounter is ongoing budget maintenance. While the project manager may have created the best-ever project blueprint at the start of the project, projects are not linear and never (and I do mean never) follow the initial plans. Risks and issues arise, business needs change, development pitfalls occur, all impacting the project budget. As such, it is critical that the project manager not only documents every issue but also remains diligent about the actual project costs consumed and future cost projections. Any issue that could materially impact the project budget should be escalated to the project sponsor before the costs are realized. The project sponsor will provide guidance on how to navigate the situation to remain as close to budget as possible. If a significant development occurs that will materially impact the budget, the project manager may need to appeal to finance for additional funding which may or may not get approved.

Project Budgets That Extend to Multiple Fiscal Periods

The last budget issue project managers must be aware of relates to projects that begin during one fiscal period but end in another. Department budgets in U.S. banks get refreshed according to the bank's fiscal calendar, which is usually annually spanning from January 1 to December 31. Projects that begin during one fiscal period and end in another will require funding in two separate budgets—the current year and following year. For example, if a project begins in June of the current year and is expected to last through March of the following year, budgets for the current year will get closed at December month-end and a new one will begin in January. As such, the project manager must ensure the project has secured funding in the current year budget as well in the next year's budget. Failure to do so could end up with a major shortfall in the project budget that would require emergency funding, or a discontinuation of the project altogether, neither of which is a desirable outcome.

Political Issues

At some point in time, all project managers experience some level of political pressure that will impact the project in one way or another. As political pressure can come from any direction at any time, it cannot be predicted or expected, only planned for. Examples of political pressure include individual differences in opinion about the bank's strategy, goals, product mix, and so on that could seriously derail a project or in a worst-case scenario render a project entirely obsolete. Seismic shifts in key dynamics such as bank strategy during a project are uncommon so the project manager should not spend time planning for such an event. If that event should occur, the project manager should pause and reevaluate the project along with the project sponsor to determine if the project remains relevant.

More common examples of political pressure come in the form of differences in opinion on mostly subjective issues that cannot be resolved without escalation. Deciding on the best technological solution, the best way to finance a project, the best way to avoid scope creep (bunding new business requirements with existing business requirements with the hope of gaining business efficiency or reduced development costs), the best legal advice, and so on. "The best" is always subjective but when dealing with dominant, alpha-business personalities commonly found in banking upper management, there is rarely 100 percent consensus on the best of anything. In these instances, the project manager must first escalate to the project sponsor and continue to escalate the issue until resolution. As the issue is passed to higher levels of management, the project manager should remain neutral and well versed in all project matters. The issue will eventually be decided upon by someone in management who is in a position that directly or indirectly has the authority to make overarching decisions and would not need further escalation as doing so would be professionally detrimental to all involved.

Whether the issues of managing a bank project are strategic, technological, budgetary, or political, a bank project manager must have some subject matter expertise in the project, be a strong communicator, and deliver results. Over time, a bank project manager with a good reputation for doing all of these things will be in high demand for the foreseeable future.

Organizational Structure

While there are at least as many types of organizational structures as there are organizations, how each bank's organization is structured has a direct impact on how projects are managed. Does the project manager have little to no authority, some authority, or complete authority over the project he/she manages? Is there a dedicated PMO (project management office) that centralizes all project management authority? Do project sponsors and business lines recognize the project manager's role or is the project manager not taken seriously?

The Project Management Institute identifies three major organizational types: functional, matrix, and projectized. A functional organizational structure is hierarchal in nature where reporting lines go up creating a Λ shaped organizational chart and business line are identified by specialty such as marketing, accounting, and so on. In a projectized organizational structure, project managers are highly independent and exert a significant amount of influence over a project. Lastly, a matrix organizational structure is a combination of both a functional and projectized organization. It is not uncommon for a single company to employ multiple organizational structures throughout the firm to achieve desired results. (*A Guide to the Project Management Body of Knowledge* (*PMBOK Guide*) 5th edition 2013). Whatever the organizational structure is, the project manager must be aware of the structure to maximize the project's overall value.

Nature of the Project

In order to reach the bank's tactical short-term and strategic long-term objectives, projects are often grouped into programs (a collection of projects geared to a specific objective) and programs are grouped into portfolios (a collection of programs to achieve strategic objectives). The nature of each project will determine how each project is managed as not all projects are the same. For illustrative purposes, this chapter will demonstrate how a U.S. bank regulatory, IT, new product offering, or new policy implementation project may be managed. It is important to note that projects can fall into multiple or all these categories, so the project manager needs to be well versed in the process for each.

Regulatory Project

A regulatory project is one in which the bank's governing institution has cited the bank for violation of one or more bank regulations and the bank needs to resolve the issue. These types of projects require documentation for everything that is involved in the project including but not limited to scope documents, project management meeting minutes, steering committee meeting minutes, executive committee meeting minutes, project plans, project budgets, business requirements, technical specifications, and evidence of stakeholder approval for each phase of the project lifecycle. This evidence will be provided to regulators to prove the problem the bank was cited for has been resolved. As such, regulatory projects require a significant amount of project administration and organization.

IT Project

A bank IT project is typically one in which there is a new software program that is being built or purchased and must be fully integrated with the bank's existing technological infrastructure. The focus on these projects is usually project scope and development that does not require as much project administration. Documents such as a project charter (high-level description of the project), business requirements, functional specifications (how the solution should work), and project timeline is where the project manager spends most of his or her time.

New Product Offering

A new product offering project requires a lot of research and coordination. Research is done on a group of people or businesses to determine what new product or product feature warrants development and offering. Once the research is complete, the project manager must coordinate efforts between marketing, operations, finance, legal, human resources, and potentially IT teams to develop and implement the product. Marketing materials have to be created and distributed, operations people have to be trained on the product and be ready to answer questions, finance has to pay for it, legal has to approve it, human resources needs to identify new employees, and IT teams need to build it. Smaller banks will have only one project manager to coordinate all these activities while larger banks may have one project manager that specializes in each activity.

Policy Implementation Project

A project where a new policy has to be implemented usually does not require IT resources but instead, legal resources—people who thoroughly understand the rules and regulations that influence new bank policy, how it differs from existing bank policy, and what the bank must do to ensure it complies with the new policy once it is implemented. The project manager should have at least peripheral knowledge of legal terms or should get up to speed quickly. The administration of this type of project will be focused on writing and rewriting policies, circulating for approval, and repeating the process until all stakeholders are satisfied with the final product. While communication is essential for all projects, it is especially critical when dealing with policy projects as the wording must be precise to achieve the desired objective.

Conclusion

It is common for projects across all industries to experience similar challenges regarding strategic, technological, budgetary, and political influences. As such, one could argue that the approach to resolve these challenges will also be the same not just for banking but across industries. The best approach to manage and minimize the number of issues for any project is certainly to use a simple, easily repeatable project management process. However, existing dynamics within the banking sector require subject matter and cultural expertise in areas of banking to improve the overall project success. With time and practice, knowing what project management strategy to use and when will become second nature to the bank project manager, allowing him or her to focus on the project itself. With experience, a bank project manager should also build up a reputation of reliability, strong communication skills, and a track record of achieving results that will leave that bank project manager in demand for years to come.

CHAPTER 6

Mastering Bank Project Management Challenges

It is no secret that every project in every industry comes with its own set of challenges. The banking industry is no different. Whether the bank wants to replace aging legacy systems, offer a new product, reduce operating costs, increase revenue, or bolster its compliance program, the projects created to accomplish these goals will undoubtedly experience challenges. So, the question is not if the project will experience challenges but when and what can the project manager do about it.

This chapter will offer ways to master bank project management challenges with a focus on sponsor/stakeholder challenges, communication challenges, and risk management challenges.

Project Sponsor/Stakeholder Challenges

The bank project sponsor is most often the senior business manager expected to receive the benefits of the completed project. Keeping with that logic, it makes complete sense since the project sponsor would then, by default, have the most at stake in the project as he or she has a vested interest in the overall success of the project. However, there are inherent flaws with this logic since the project sponsor may be, "…a 'butterfly sponsor' with uneven interest in a project, a 'reluctant sponsor', who is not committed to the intended benefits from the project, or even an 'incompetent sponsor' who does not understand the role" (Richard Breese 2020).

In their research on the topic, Breese, Couch, and Turner (2020) identified three conceptions of the project sponsor role, how the project sponsor defined "realized benefits," and delimited role of the project sponsor depicted in the following chart (Richard Breese 2020):

Table 6.1 Project Sponsor's Benefits Realization Model

Sponsor's focus	Project sponsor's definition of "realization benefits"	Delimiting role of project sponsor
Just doing the day job	Did not recognize any benefits realization	Figure head role
The capable manager	Identifies benefits as part of delivering projects	The scope of personal authority and experience
Wearing two different hats (business manager and project manager)	Identifies benefits and understands responsibilities for realizing them as part of role	Collective ownership with a defined structure

The research supports the notion that the project sponsor who views his/her role as "wearing two different hats" such that the project management responsibilities are separate from running the daily business recognizes the benefits the of the project and takes responsibility for the project success. The problem is in banking project management, the project sponsor is often "just doing the day job," is only a figure head, and therefore, not realizing the benefits of the project or project management process. So how should the bank project manager master this challenge?

The answer is entrenched in understanding why the problem of a sponsor as only a figure head exists in the first place. Senior managers in the banking industry carved their teeth on a grindstone that did not include project managers, defined project management practices or philosophies, or an appreciation for the benefits a well-managed project can bring; there was a job to do, he or she got the job done consistently over time and elevated to the roles they are in now. The approach to master this challenge is easily remembered using the mnemonic: show the project sponsor MERCI—meet, educate, report, communicate, and induce.

Meeting with the project sponsor regularly may not be easy since he or she is a senior person with a business to run. The project manager must be persistent in these efforts as there is no better way to explain the ins and outs of a project with the project sponsor than in person.

Educate the project sponsor on everything related to project management from the types of documents that he or she will be required to approve, why, and how it influences the overall project process. The project sponsor should also be educated on project risks, issues, budgets, critical dates in the project plan, and any other aspect of the project he or she may be unaware of.

Report progress to the project sponsor regularly. This should be weekly at a minimum and can be easily completed each Friday as an "end-of-week project recap." These reports should not replace the in-person meetings but should supplement the information shared during those meetings. Reporting should also include test results, performance metrics, and project meeting minutes for all project meetings even if the project sponsor was in attendance.

Communicate with the project sponsor outside of in-person meetings and weekly recap reports. Issues arise sometimes daily and having a timely conversation with a project sponsor can mitigate project risk, overcome project challenges, or provide guidance when a solution is uncertain.

Induce the project sponsor to act when needed. The project sponsor's approval is required for many project management documents, business requirements, change control logs, budget items, and user acceptance testing results to name a few. A project sponsor should also be induced to act when the project is at an impasse and requires a senior member of the bank to weigh in. Having MERCI on your project sponsor will certainly enhance the probability of realizing project benefits.

Communication Challenges

There is overwhelming research supporting the criticality of good communication to reach business goals or achieve project success. Research conducted by the Project Management Institute turned the issue around to better understand the impact of poor communication. The research estimates that two out of every five projects fail and out of those two projects that fails, one fails due to "ineffective communications" (Project Management Institute 2013). Stating the problem differently, it is estimated that 20 percent of projects fail due to communication problems. This section will identify the types of communications problems a bank project manager encounters most often and how to master communication challenges.

Use Appropriate Language

It is easy for a project manager to get wrapped up in the language used to describe various aspects of project management when describing the process to others. It is important to be aware that while it may be common knowledge to an experienced project manager what a work breakdown structure is, what the critical path of a project is, or what enterprise environmental factors are, stakeholders such as the project sponsor, management, or even other members of the project team may not be aware of them. Imagine what it would sound like if a doctor explained to you in medical terminology what is wrong with you and how to treat it; you would not understand any of it. As such, it is always best to use common terms that your stakeholders are familiar with without being overly technical. If it cannot be avoided, then you as the project manager have an obligation to educate stakeholders what you are referring to and why before moving on to another topic.

For example, if you had to describe what a work breakdown structure is to someone with no project management experience, you could go to your *PMBOK Guide*, flip to the glossary, and look it up. If you read the definition of a work breakdown structure out loud, you would say, "A work breakdown structure is a hierarchical decomposition of the total scope of work to be carried out by the project team to accomplish the project objectives and create the required deliverables" (*A Guide to the Project Management Body of Knowledge* (*PMBOK Guide*) 5th edition 2013) Wait, what? Saying it more simply, a work breakdown structure is basically a list of things that need to get done. That is simplifying it quite a bit but everyone around the table can understand and relate to that definition. The more experience a project manager has, the easier it becomes to use common terms for stakeholders to understand.

Know Your Audience

What does it mean to know your audience? It means that you have a firm grasp of all the dynamics in play when speaking to one or many people regarding your project management updates. The dynamics in play include how many people are in your audience, what levels of the organization the individual members of your audience belong to, and how familiar they are regarding the project you are discussing. Your audience may be one person or many. In a one-on-one setting, you audience could be a project management peer, your project sponsor, your line manager, a higher-level manager, and so on. In a broader forum, your audience may include your entire project team, a committee, the development team, and other groups of internal or external stakeholders. Once you know your audience, you can then tailor your project management updates accordingly by understanding what the key message is you want to convey, the language you should use to convey it, and the appropriate level of detail to include when conveying it. As an example, consider this scenario:

> During a recent two-week testing phase, 100 test scripts were executed; 80 test scripts passed, and 20 test scripts failed. Out of the 20 failed test scripts, 5 were identified as "high priority," 12 were identified as "medium priority," and three were identified as "low priority." All the high priority items were attributed to a coding error that impacted different aspects of the front end. The development team was notified of all 20 failures and are actively fixing each one, beginning with high priority and moving toward low priority. It is estimated that the critical items will be fixed and ready for testing in one week while the remaining 15 medium and low priority items will be fixed and ready for testing in two weeks. The development team is confident that all items will be fixed without issue with no negative impact to the project budget or timeline. As such, the project remains on schedule for Q4 implementation.

Based on the above scenario, here are examples of how to communicate this information to various audiences:

- Executive Manager with limited project knowledge: "The project is currently in a testing phase and remains on track for Q4 implementation."
- Line Manager with detailed project knowledge: "During the first round of testing, 20 test scripts failed with five of those

items identified as critical. We should be able to retest all items within the next two weeks. If those tests are successful, the project remains on track for Q4 implementation."

- Project Sponsor: "During the first round of testing, 20 test scripts failed with five of them identified as critical. The developers identified a coding error that impacted different aspects of the front end, but we should be able to retest those items in one week and retest the other items in two weeks. If all tests are successful, the project remains on track for a Q4 implementation."
- Project Team: All the information in the scenario should be shared with the project team including detailed descriptions of the failed tests and proposed solutions. The project team should actively test the corrections, report the outcomes, and communicate any risks or issues encountered.

A good general rule of thumb is that as you go up in the organization, the message communicated should get shorter, be focused on the critical information, and described using common language. If the person or persons you are speaking to want more information, he or she will ask for it.

Communicate Strategic and Business Benefits of the Project

To ensure ongoing engagement from the project team and maintain a high probability for project success, the project manager must ensure that all project team members fully understand the strategic and/or business benefits of executing the prescribed project. If there is any breakdown in this communication, the project team will question the validity of the project, disengage from the project, or neglect the project altogether. This leads to project discourse, resulting in major breakdowns on several key project management processes, and significantly increases the risk of project failure.

The best way to master this challenge is for the project manager to be clear on the value add of the project even before the project kicks off and reinforce the message throughout the project management process.

The best source to derive this information from is the project sponsor as he or she is usually fully engrained in the business, understands what the business needs to improve, and can articulate how fixing the problem will help the business. As such, the project sponsor will communicate the value add, but not the how; that will be up to the project manager.

Risks Management Challenges

When discussing project management processes, the discussion of risks and issues usually go together. As such, to fully understand how to master project risks management, it is important to understand the difference between risks and issues. The easiest way to think of a risk is something that threatens an aspect of your project that has not happened yet, whereas an issue threatens the project, and either is happening or has already happened. As such, both risks and issues need to be managed differently.

Risks

Project risks are varied, elusive, and difficult to identify and manage for any project. In banking, the biggest risks a project manager needs to be most concerned with are those risks that could affect the project timeline, performance failures, or project budget. While this section will focus on these risks, the reader should be aware this is not a comprehensive list of risks that could impact banking projects.

The most common risks that could negatively impact a project timeline are availability of resources. The availability of resources means there are enough human resources available throughout the entirety of the project and have the right skillset to execute the project. Risks that could impact the availability of resources include issues such as a global pandemic, people leave the firm or are reassigned, maternity and paternity time off, extended sick time, unexpected corporate downsizing, or the inability to find human resources with a desired skillset. Essentially, any issue that could impact the availability of human resources to the project, if materialized, will impact the project timeline.

Performance failures could be due to issues such as miscommunication in requirements, a lack of skills on either the project side or development side of project execution, a lack of adequate technology to solve the problem, or budget constraints that do not allow further investment in the project. The result could be a final product that does not meet specifications, only solves part of the initial problem, or in a worst-case scenario is considered throw away and the project is scrapped altogether.

The biggest risk to bank project budgets is project scope. Determining the appropriate solution to a problem can be a straightforward process, particularly if high-quality analysis was performed on the issue. What is more difficult to understand from the beginning of a project is to know exactly what needs to be fixed and how. Subject matter experts are consulted to give their opinion on the issue and that forms the basis for project requirements. However, once a deep dive into the issue is undertaken, the result usually ends up being an expanded project scope that will undoubtedly increase the project budget and inevitably the project timeline.

In order to master these and other bank project risks, the Project Management Institute has a comprehensive approach that when used properly will help the project manager identify, manage, and resolve project risks, greatly improving the probability of project success. The framework for the project risk management process is as follows: (*A Guide to the Project Management Body of Knowledge* (*PMBOK Guide*) 5th edition 2013).

- Plan Risk Management—a plan created by the project manager detailing how he or she will manage risk
- Identify Risks—determine which risks will affect the project
- Perform Qualitative Risk Analysis—prioritizing risks identified in the previous step based on probability of occurrence and impact
- Perform Quantitative Risk Analysis—calculating what the impact of the identified risks could be on the outcome of the project
- Plan Risk Responses—a plan on how to deal with these risks as they arise and how the project manager will communicate risk responses to the project team

- Control Risks—implement risk response plans, track identified risks, look for other risks, and consistently evaluate the risk process effectiveness throughout the life of the project

The example below will reinforce how to use this framework.

A project manager is in the planning phase of a project to upgrade an aging bank legacy system. The project is expected to take one year, and the budget is capped at $250,000. There will be three technology developers and two project team members assigned for the duration of the project, although one project team member is up for promotion in six months and could be taken off the project if the promotion goes through. During the planning phase, the project manager considers what risks may arise on the project and how he will deal with those risks.

Using the framework above, the project manager should consider the following:

- Plan Risk Management—the project manager should be conscious of the fact he has five people on the project, one potentially leaving in six months, determine if each person has the proper skillset for this project, monitor closely what the baseline scope is so the project budget does not go over $250,000, and monitor any issues that could arise that would push the project timeline over one year.
- Identify Risks—the person up for promotion is a risk and not knowing what the skillset is of each person is a risk; the project manager documents these risks in a risk register in order to monitor the risk and add new risks if needed.
- Perform Qualitative Risk Analysis—the project manager prioritizes the risk of losing a project team member since he estimates there is a 50 percent change the person will be promoted, followed by a 10 percent chance there is a mismatch in skillset with one or more of the project team members.

- Perform Quantitative Risk Analysis—the project manager creates a probability and impact matrix to determine what level the risks are from low, medium, to high.
- Plan Risk Responses—The project manager submits a request for a contract employee to join the team in six months in the event the project team member is promoted. The project manager describes the skillset required for the contract employee to make sure there is a match between the potential open role and candidate.
- Control Risks—the project manager allocates time in his weekly project meetings to discuss any risks that are present and surveys his team if any new risks have been identified. If a new project risk is identified, it would be placed in the risk register and follow the same path as the previously identified risks.

What makes the Project Management Institute's framework most effective is that it is a simple framework that can be applied to any project, is easily replicated, and promotes good communication and risk monitoring throughout the project. When used properly for bank project risk management, it is a highly impactful tool that will increase the project's probability for success.

CHAPTER 7

Introduction to Bank Regulatory Agencies

The role of compliance in the banking industry has evolved over time due to a myriad of issues including, but not limited to, the rapid advancement of technology, changes in retail and commercial customer financial needs, and the ability of financial institutions to provide access to capital or transact anytime, anywhere in the world. In the simplest of forms, compliance organizations within a financial institution were tasked with policing activities of the firm and issuing policies and procedures aligned to regulatory recommendations. That approach is no longer acceptable as banking compliance organizations are now expected to not only police bank activities while issuing policies and procedures in line with regulatory recommendations but also to actively manage and mitigate risk related to employees, products, services, customers, customers' customers, vendors, and so on.

There is no shortage of regulatory bodies within the United States that are tasked with preserving, maintaining, and ensuring the stability and integrity of the banking industry. Understanding the roles and responsibilities of each can be a laborious, time-consuming process. As such, this chapter will focus on specific regulatory bodies that oversee various aspects of the U.S. banking industry including the Office of the Comptroller of the Currency (OCC), the Federal Reserve System, the Federal Deposit Insurance Company (FDIC), the U.S. Securities and Exchange Commission (SEC), the Office of Foreign Assets Control (OFAC), the National Credit Union Administration (NCUA), the Office of Thrift Supervision (OTS), and the Consumer Financial Protection Bureau (CFPB).

The Office of the Comptroller of the Currency (OCC)

Abraham Lincoln signed the National Currency Act into Law on February 25, 1863, which created the OCC. Abraham Lincoln knew the importance of having a stable monetary and banking system, particularly with the threat of war on the horizon and a need to fund its efforts. The OCC quickly established a formal banking system along with a stable paper currency, both of which were critical to achieve both short-term (war funding) and long-term (depositing, redeeming, or exchanging bank notes) economic goals outlined by Lincoln himself (Founding of the OCC and the National Banking System 2020). In a strategic move, Lincoln appointed Hugh McCulloch as the first Comptroller of the Currency, who was not in favor of a national banking system as he felt it was a threat to state and local banks. However, under his leadership, McCulloch chartered 868 banks in his first 22 months with zero failures (Hugh McCulloch, the First Comptroller 2020).

In terms of governance, the OCC, "charters, regulates, and supervises all national banks and federal savings associations as well as federal branches and agencies of foreign banks. The OCC is an independent bureau of the U.S. Department of the Treasury and is led by the Comptroller of the Currency" (Organization 2020). Essentially, the OCC is an independent entity within the U.S. Treasury that supervises, regulates, and enforces regulations found in the federal banking charters for both banks and savings institutions as well as issues licenses and provides protection to the customers of these institutions. It is by far the largest U.S. regulator of banks in both size (number of banks) and scope (banking regulations).

The Federal Reserve System

Prior to 1913, there was widespread instability within the U.S. banking industry with "panics, seasonal cash crunches, and a high rate of bank failures" (Beattie 2020). Several attempts were made to stabilize the industry to no avail until the Panic of 1907 when an earthquake in San Francisco "drew gold out of the world's money centers" (Tucker 2008) and ultimately causing a recession. Wall Street turned to J.P. Morgan to rescue the country from a potential crash and full-blown depression (sound familiar—think financial crisis of 2008). After the crisis was averted, J.P. Morgan insisted the United States create a central bank. From 1907 through 1913, top bankers from across the United States traveled to Britain and Germany, along with those of other countries whose banking industries were much more stable, to learn their banking practices. The end result culminated in then-president, Woodrow Wilson, signing the Federal Reserve Act into law, which created the current Federal Reserve System.

The Federal Reserve acts as the U.S. Central Bank and is comprised of the Federal Reserve Board of Governors tasked with overseeing the operations of the 12 Federal Reserve Banks that "store currency and coin, processing checks and electronic payments; handle the Treasury's payments, sell government securities to assist with the Treasury's cash management and investment activities, and conduct research on regional, national, and international economic issues" (Federal Reserve Education 2020) and the Federal Open Market Committee who makes monetary policy for the Federal Reserve System.

According to the Federal Reserve's website (federalreserve.gov), the Federal Reserve "performs five general functions to promote effective operation of the U.S. economy, and more generally, the public interest.

1. Conducts the nation's monetary policy to promote maximum employment, stable prices, and moderate long-term interest rates in the U.S. economy;
2. Promotes stability of the financial system and seeks to minimize and contain systemic risks through active monitoring and engagement in the U.S. and abroad;
3. Promotes the safety and soundness of individual financial institutions and monitors their impact on the financial system as a whole;
4. Fosters payment and settlement system safety and efficiency through services to the banking industry and the U.S. government that facilitate U.S.-dollar transactions and payments; and
5. Promotes consumer protection and community development through consumer-focused supervision and examination, research and analysis of emerging consumer issues and trends, community economic development activities, and the administration of consumer laws and regulations" (About the Fed 2020) (Figure 7.1).

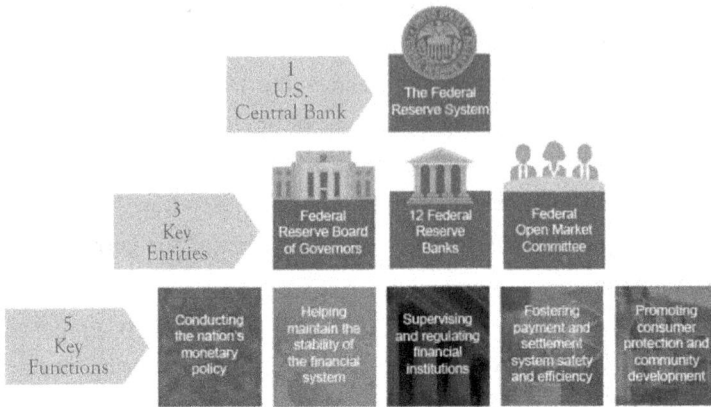

Figure 7.1 Structure of federal reserve system

Source: The Federal Reserve Website.

The Federal Deposit Insurance Corporation (FDIC)

The U.S. banking system struggled to find solid footing beginning with the establishment of the U.S. government in 1776. Factors contributing to the banking system woes included an unstable banking system, an unstable currency, and widespread bank failures during multiple economic crises. U.S. politicians tried various ways to curtail the problem to no avail as people would scramble to withdraw money from banks the moment an economic crisis seemed imminent. This caused many bank failures since there was no insurance on peoples' deposits.

The U.S. banking system continued to struggle mightily during the Great Depression from 1929 until 1933 as the United States witnessed record-breaking bank failures. Then on March 4, 1933, Franklin Roosevelt took office as the elected president of the United States and on June 16, 1933, signed the Banking Act of 1933 (the act) into law. This was an enormous step forward toward assisting the banking system difficulties as the act created, at least on a temporary basis, the Federal Deposit Insurance Corporation (FDIC), which insured customers' money up to a certain threshold. For the first time in U.S. history, customers did not have to worry about losing money if a bank should become insolvent. The FDIC would become a permanent fixture in U.S. banking history with the signing of the Banking Act of 1935.

There are two basic functions of the FDIC: to protect consumer funds and instill confidence in the U.S. banking system. The FDIC protects customer funds by mandating that banks who wish to be FDIC insured pay premiums into an insurance fund. "With numerous banks paying premiums, the cost of bank failures is shared and spread out over time" (*Understanding the FDIC: Overview of History of the Federal Deposit Insurance Corporation* 2020). The FDIC will also monitor banks to ensure each institution is not taking unnecessary risks since the deposits will be "protected" in the event of a failure.

In addition to providing insurance on deposits, the FDIC also protects consumers by working with the OCC, Federal Reserve, and National Credit Union Association to regulate the U.S. banking system, as well as provides resources to communities for additional consumer protection. For example, the FDIC strives to educate consumers on their rights, provides a monthly newsletter, and works in local communities encouraging banks to meet the needs of the people in those communities.

The Security and Exchange Commission (SEC)

Anyone who has sat through a U.S. History class in high school is well aware of the "roaring 20's" (1920s), a period in U.S. history of a searing hot economy and widespread prosperity. However, the economy began to shift in August of 1929 and on Monday, October 24,1929, also known as "Black Monday," the Dow Jones Industrial Average fell nearly 13 percent, followed by "Black Tuesday" when the exchange plunged another 13 percent. This contributed to what is known in U.S. history as "The Great Depression."

What is lesser known about that time period are the exact causes that triggered the downturn, be it rising interest rates, people who were over levered in a rising interest rate environment, economic pressure on the American farmer, all of these issues, and possibly other issues. Panic ensued, there was a run on banks as people scrambled to withdraw their money, banks and businesses went bankrupt, and unemployment skyrocketed. State-run banks and businesses did a poor job of regulating themselves and so it was left to the U.S. government to intervene.

Then in 1932, Franklin Delano Roosevelt stated during his Democratic Party nomination acceptance speech that he wanted tighter regulation on the securities industry. After being elected president in 1933, the Securities Act of 1933 went into effect on May 27, 1933. The act accomplished two main goals: it made the federal government the official regulators of the securities industry, no longer residing within the states, and forced stock issuing companies to provide full disclosure about the company to potential investors. The following year, U.S. Congress passed the Securities Exchange Act of 1934, which created the Securities and Exchange Commission (SEC).

The SEC is tasked with a "three part mission: protect investors, maintain fair, orderly and efficient markets, and facilitate capital formation" (The Role of the SEC 2020) What does that statement really mean though? In its simplest form, the SEC is tasked with making sure companies looking to sell stock to investors provide comprehensive information about its financial ongoings and business dealings so a potential investor can decide for themselves if it is a good investment or not. The SEC also regulates those involved in the stock selling process including brokerages, investment advisors, and mutual funds, and lastly, the SEC ensures that markets in which stocks are purchased and sold are run fairly and efficiently to provide so those looking to gain access to capital are confident someone has their back in case things go wrong. In this case, the SEC, a federally operating regulator, would provide that safety.

The Office of Foreign Assets Control (OFAC)

OFAC was created in December of 1950 by then-president, Harry S. Truman. OFAC's mission is to administer and enforce "economic and trade sanctions based on U.S. foreign policy and national security goals against targeted foreign countries and regimes, terrorists, international narcotics traffickers, those engaged in activities related to the proliferation of weapons of mass destruction, and other threats to the national security, foreign policy of economy of the United States" (U.S. Department of Treasury: Mission 2020). OFAC was essentially tasked with regulating trade with any country or person that posed a threat to the national interest of the United States.

U.S. sanctions against foreign countries dates back to the time between the end of the American Revolution in 1783 and the War of 1812 when the U.S. Department of the Treasury imposed sanctions on Great Britain for harassing U.S. sailors. Sanctions were used once again during the Civil War, preventing the North from engaging in trade with the South, applying economic pressure on the South. Sanctions were used yet again during World War II to prevent Nazi Germany from engaging in any foreign trade, which was an effective tool at limiting Germany's economic capabilities.

Finally, in 1950, after China entered into the Korean War, President Truman, "declared a national emergency and blocked all Chinese and North Korean assets subject to U.S. jurisdiction" (U.S. Department of Treasury: History). OFAC, which was a successor to the Foreign Funds Control (FFC), became a division of the U.S. Department of the Treasury tasked with regulating all foreign economic and trade policies. Since that time, OFAC has established itself as a well-known, powerful government agency capable of levying significant penalties against those that disregard its directives.

The National Credit Union Administration (NCUA)

The first credit union in the United States was formed on April 6, 1909 by the St. Mary's Cooperative Association. Prior to that, credit unions originated in the late nineteenth century by Europeans as part of the "cooperatives" movement. Cooperatives were different groups of people who banded together to achieve a common goal. The idea of establishing a "credit union" evolved from the cooperatives who wanted to pool their money together in order to reach certain financial goals, such as building a house or starting a business. As the number of cooperatives across the United States increased, and in turn the number of credit unions increased, the need for regulation of credit unions became apparent after the Great Depression of the 1930s.

From the 1930s to 1960s, various regulations were passed to benefit the credit unions and helped them increase in size and numbers. By 1960, there were over 9,900 credit unions in the United States, with 6.1 million members and $2.7 billion in assets (National Credit

Union Association: Historical Timeline 2020). It became the goal of the credit unions to expand into low- to moderate-income areas in order to improve the economic conditions within those communities. However, there was no federal regulation of the credit unions as it resided largely within the states.

That would change by 1970 with the creation of the NCUA, an independent federal agency to oversee federal credit unions. One major component of that legislation was the establishment of an insurance fund, the National Credit Union Share Insurance Fund, that provided federal insurance on credit union deposits up to $20,000. Prior to the legislation, credit union deposits were not insured by the federal government.

There are four basic directives carried out by the NCUA:

1. Insure deposits made at federal credit unions;
2. Provide licenses for credit unions to operate (called charters);
3. Regulate credit unions within the United States; and
4. Monitor all federally chartered credit union activity (Payne 2020).

The Office of Thrift Supervision (OTS)

The history of the OTS dates back to 1932 when the Federal Home Loan Bank Act (FHLBA) was created with the intent of making home ownership a reality for more Americans. The country was in the midst of the Great Depression, many Americans who had mortgages were defaulting on payments, and the housing market was suffering tremendously due to the aggregation of these circumstances. Passing the FHLBA was a way for the U.S. government to inject money into the banking system intended to boost the housing market.

The passage of the FHLBA also created the Federal Home Loan Bank Board and Federal Home Loan Banks. "The Federal Home Loan Bank Board chartered and managed Federal Savings and Loan Banks and organizations" (Kagan 2020). The Board was given $125 million to disburse to savings and loan companies, thrifts (a type of bank that specializes in savings accounts and home mortgages), insurance companies, and others to be available for home mortgages.

If you fast forward to the 1970s, there was a toxic combination of high interest rates, low economic growth, and high inflation. People responded by withdrawing their money from low-interest paying banks to invest in higher interest paying money market funds. In order to remain competitive, savings and loans institutions began taking on higher risk by investing in commercial real estate and junk bonds. These factors culminated into what is known as the "Savings and Loan Crisis" of the 1980s. "Widespread corruption and other factors led to the insolvency of the Federal Savings and Loan Insurance Corporation, the $124 billion bailout of junk bond investments, and the liquidation of more than 700 Savings and Loans by the Resolution Trust Corporation" (Kenton 2019).

In response to the Savings and Loan crisis, the OTS was created in 1989 as a successor to the Federal Home Loan Bank Board. The OTS was now "the primary federal regulator of all federal and state-chartered savings institutions across the nation" (U.S. Department of the Treasury: History 2020). As the federal regulator of savings institutions, the OTS are tasked with issuing charters for institutions and ensure those institutions operate in a safe and efficient manner.

The Consumer Financial Protection Bureau

Just as in other times of financial crisis when the U.S. federal government was forced to intervene, the Consumer Financial Protection Bureau was born out of another financial crisis. This time, it was the housing market crash of 2007–2008. With easy access to credit, "widespread failures in consumer protection and rapid growth in irresponsible lending practices, many lenders took advantage of the gaps in consumer protection by selling mortgages and other products that were overly complicated" (Consumer Financial Protection Bureau, n.d.). Mortgage holders saw the value of their homes plummet, people lost their jobs, and the default rate on mortgages skyrocketed. The U.S. economy was once again thrust into financial turmoil, forcing the federal government to take action.

In response to the crisis, then-president Barack Obama signed what is known as the "Dodd–Frank Wall Street Reform and Consumer Protection Act," which created the Consumer Financial Protection Bureau (CFPB). The core functions of the CFPB include:

- "Rooting out unfair, deceptive, or abusive acts by writing rules, supervising companies, and enforcing the law
- Enforcing laws that outlaw discrimination in consumer finance
- Taking customer complaints
- Enhancing financial education
- Researching the consumer experience of using financial products
- Monitoring financial markets for new risks to consumers" (CFPB Consumer Financial Protection Bureau 2020)

The main benefits of the CFPB include "stronger consumer financial markets, increased transparency in the marketplace, and established necessary safeguards against predatory lending practices" (Joint Economic Committee 2020). From a financial standpoint, the CFPB provided almost $12 billion in relief and reduced consumer debt by $7.7 billion.

Summary

When you consider the history of the United States and couple it with the history of the financial system within the United States, it can be likened to that of a startup company. The business idea is formed, money is needed to keep the engine turning, there are several missteps along the way, economic conditions force the company to pivot in response to those conditions, you grow in size and maturity, and learn from mistakes. That is how the history of the U.S. financial system has played out.

The argument could be made that at only 244 years old, the United States has not fully matured from a startup to a stable organization, but it is close. It is critical that the U.S. government continues to monitor and enforce the ongoings of the financial system, protect consumers of the financial system, and balance the amount of regulation with sound business practices within the financial system, to maintain the faith and credibility of those around the world who interact with the U.S. financial system.

CHAPTER 8

Introduction to Bank Compliance Regulations

Since the inception of the United States as a country 1776, the U.S. financial system has experienced many changes as it first struggled to find solid footing as an inefficient process with an unstable currency. After many failed and successful attempts to fix the most prevalent issues, the U.S. financial system has evolved into one of the most important financial systems in the world economy as transactions are backed in full faith by the federal government. This process transformed over hundreds of years with the creation of both regulatory bodies as well as regulations themselves.

With an increase in the speed of technology, the ability to transact globally in real time, and the ever-progressing threats to the U.S. financial system, it is critical that both regulators and regulations adapt to these lightning-quick dynamics. As such, this chapter will focus on some of the most prevalent banking regulations governing the financial industry today.

Financial Recordkeeping and Reporting of Currency and Foreign Transactions Act

The Financial Recordkeeping and Reporting of Currency and Foreign Transactions Act of 1970, also known as the Bank Secrecy Act (BSA), was created to curb the increase in organized crime, particularly drug trafficking and tax evasion, that rose steadily throughout the 1960s. The BSA consists of two parts: "Title I Financial Recordkeeping and Title II Reports of Currency and Foreign Transactions" (Bank Secrecy Act 2020) and was "designed to help identify the source, volume, and movement of currency and other monetary instruments transported or transmitted into or out of the U.S." (Stackhouse 2018).

Federally insured financial institutions were required to keep track of any and every single currency transaction in the amount of $10,000 or greater. "A currency transaction is any transaction involving the physical transfer of currency from one person to another and covers deposits, withdrawals, exchanges, or transfers of currency or other payments" (Bank Secrecy Act, Anti-Money Laundering, and Office of Foreign Assets Control 2020). Financial institutions would complete what is known as a Currency Transaction Report (CTR) and submit to the Financial Crimes Enforcement Network, also known as FinCEN, which was created in 1990 to bolster financial investigations.

What is fascinating about this particular piece of legislation is that it was concerned with transaction volumes and dollars but not money laundering since money laundering itself was not a crime in 1970. As such, the impact of its passing was minimal. Money laundering would not become a crime until 1986 when the BSA was updated with what is known as the "Money Laundering Control Act." The Money Laundering Control Act of 1986 made "the hiding and reinvestment of illegal profit made from a criminal enterprise a new federal offense" (Curule 1994–1995). The Money Laundering Control Act of 1986 was also not concerned with the criminal activity that generated the funds, it was concerned only with what happened to those funds as a result of the underlying criminal activity. In essence, if someone who was involved with the drug trade in 1986 could be charged for drug-related crimes under the appropriate drug-related statues, and then additional charges of money laundering if and only if that same person attempted to hide the source and use of the funds generated from the drug activity.

From 1986 to the present time, amendments were made to the BSA. In an effort to stay ahead of the criminal curve and assist with the deterrence, investigation, and identification of financial crimes, as well as the introduction of new legislation in direct response to financial environmental factors. The following regulations are a subset of some of the most prevalent regulations impacting U.S. financial institutions as well as U.S. bank compliance programs.

The Annunzio-Wylie Anti-Money Laundering Act of 1992

The Annunzio-Wylie Anti-Money Laundering Act of 1992 introduced increased penalties for money laundering crimes, including the death penalty and civil penalties, the inclusion of sire transfers into the regulation that were previously largely unregulated, the requirement for "depository institutions to identify their customers and financial institutions with which they do business, even if the later do not hold accounts with the bank" (Morgan 1997) and the requirement for financial institutions to file suspicious activity reports (SARs) on transactions over $5,000 if the institution believes the funds are a direct or indirect result of illegal activity.

Two components of the Annunzio-Wylie Anti-Money Laundering Act require additional focus due to the impact it had on past and present financial regulations. The first is the requirement to report on the identity of customers and who they do business with as that is the foundation for more modern know-your-client (KYC) regulation. The second is for the requirement for financial institutions to file SARs. The SAR requirement was put in place to help with investigations of financial crimes but logically it would not make sense for a financial institution to file a SAR as it would call attention to potential defects in its compliance program. To remove the inhibition to file a SAR, the legislation includes a "safe harbor" provision protecting the bank, directors, officers, and employees from liability of any wrongdoing. SARs continue to be filed by financial institutions to this day.

The Money Laundering Suppression Act of 1994

The main focus of the Money Laundering Suppression Act of 1994 was to consolidate and improve investigations into money laundering activities. On one hand, financial institutions were encouraged to "improve AML training, develop anti-money laundering examination procedures, and improve procedures for reporting suspicious activities to law enforcement" (Laumann 2019). On another hand, the U.S.

Treasury's Office of Financial Enforcement was merged with FinCEN, expanding the mission and authority of FinCEN when investigating financial crimes.

The United and Strengthening America by Providing Appropriate Tools Required to Intercept and Obstruct Terrorism Act (USA PATRIOT Act)

The USA PATRIOT Act was passed in 2001 as a direct response to the terrorist attacks on the World Trade Center and Pentagon on September 11, 2001. The regulation itself was broad and deep, and came with some controversy, particularly in areas that expanded government surveillance capabilities. In order to push the regulation through, a five-year expiry period was placed on some of the most controversial aspects of the law, providing a buffer for the federal government to enact new regulations or just let the current ones expire.

Below is an itemization of regulations stemming from the USA PATRIOT Act according to the FinCEN website:

- "Criminalized the financing of terrorism and augmented the existing BSA framework by strengthening customer identification procedures
- Prohibited financial institutions from engaging in business with foreign shell banks (a shell bank is a bank that does not have any physical presence)
- Required financial institutions to have due diligence procedures (and enhanced due diligence procedures for foreign correspondent and private banking accounts)
- Improved information sharing between financial institutions and the U.S. government by requiring government-institution information sharing and voluntary information sharing among financial institutions
- Expanded the anti-money laundering program requirements to all financial institutions
- Increased civil and criminal penalties for money laundering

- Provided the Secretary of the Treasury with the authority to impose 'special measures' on jurisdictions, institutions, or transactions that are of 'primary money laundering concern'
- Facilitated records access and required banks to respond to regulatory requests for information within 120 hours
- Required federal banking agencies to consider a bank's AML record when reviewing bank mergers, acquisitions, and other applications for business combinations" (History of Anti-Money Laundering Laws 2020).

The most controversial aspects of the USA PATRIOT Act were part of Title II: Enhanced surveillance procedures. This title afforded the U.S. government to gather "foreign intelligence information" from both U.S. and non-U.S. citizens, as well as expand the scope and availability of wiretapping. However, the most controversial provisions included "sneak and peek warrants, roving wiretaps, and the ability of the FBI to gain access to documents that reveal the patterns of U.S. citizens" (Patriot Act 2020). Sneak and peek warrants allowed law enforcement to enter the private premises without the owners' permission, roving wiretaps allowed law enforcement to follow a person via telecommunications even if a phone was thrown away and a new one activated, and allowing the FBI to access documents such as books, records, papers, and other items for an investigation. These aspects of the USA PATRIOT Act were subject to much criticism and debate in future revisions.

At around the same time the USA PATRIOT Act was passed, then-president, George W. Bush passed an executive order that "prohibited companies from conducting business with individuals or organizations labeled as terrorists" (Stephen 2005), placing them on a list known as "Specially Designated Nationals" (SDNs). On a daily basis, U.S. financial institutions must "screen transactions," meaning it filters through the names and countries in a transaction to see if there is a match on the SDN list. If there is a "hit" on a transaction, OFAC has procedures the financial institution must follow to isolate and cancel the transaction if it is in violation of the SDN criteria. The list of SDNs continues to be updated regularly and financial institutions must screen transactions against the list daily.

In order to better understand what the implications of the USA PATRIOT Act was on U.S. financial institutions, further analysis is required. Most notably, U.S. financial institutions were now required to establish its own anti-money laundering program. Interestingly enough, the guidelines set forth by financial regulators was that the anti-money laundering program need only to meet the requirements set forth in the regulation. In other words, no guidance was given on exactly how to set up an anti-money laundering program, only that the underlying activities created by the anti-money laundering program satisfied the components of the regulation. Needless to say, each U.S. financial institution applied its own methodology setting the stage for future audits by banking regulators.

In addition to establishing an anti-money laundering program, U.S. financial institutions were also required to conduct "customer due diligence" (CDD). This became known as "know your customer regulation" (KYC), where the financial institution had to not only verify that the customer is who they say they are, but that they are also being truthful about their business activities. New customers were screened during the account opening process and existing customers were recertified on a regular basis, be it every one, two, or three years depending on the risk and nature of the client's activities. There was also a need to conduct "enhanced due diligence" on politically exposed persons ("PEPs") as well as specially designated nationals (SDNs), which was a list of people identified by OFAC as being a potential threat to the United States. Banks would have to screen for PEPs and SDNs at account opening, as well as the banks' days' transactions activity.

Another well-known piece of the USA PATRIOT Act is Section 314(a) and Section 314(b). Section 314(a), "authorizes FinCEN to issue to financial institutions a list of entities and individual that are suspected of AML/CFT (combating the financing of terrorism) offenses or other criminal activities" (BSA Compliance and Section 314 2020). How it works is FinCEN submits a request for information on specific individuals or businesses. If the bank has accounts or activity on file with the people or businesses on the list, it must disclose all information to FinCEN.

Section 314(b) focuses on encouraging financial institutions to share information with one another to assist with identifying, capturing, and deterring financial crimes. Just as in other banking provisions, Section 314(b) contains safe harbor provisions allowing financial institutions to share information without fear of liability.

As with any regulation, there are penalties for violating such regulations. The U.S. government can fine an institution up to $1 million per incident, $250,000 per incident in civil fines, and the potential to be imprisoned depending on the severity of the crime. For information regarding enforcement actions taken against financial institutions, FinCEN provides this information on their website: https://fincen.gov/index.php/news-room/enforcement-actions

Dodd–Frank Wall Street Reform and Consumer Protection Act

The Dodd–Frank Wall Street Reform and Consumer Protection Act (Dodd–Frank) is a massive piece of legislation encompassing over 2,300 pages that was passed in 2010 in direct response to the financial crisis of 2008. In summary, the 2008 financial crisis was caused by extremely low interest rates, easy access to credit, people buying overpriced homes, and then lenders selling those loans to Wall Street banks as "collateralized debt obligations" (CDOs). The CDOs were packages of mortgages that took a portion of the mortgage payments made by the mortgage holder to the CDO holder in the form of interest similar to a bond. However, as interest rates climbed, default rates also climbed and the value of CDOs plummeted. Wall Street institutions were holding hundreds of billions of dollars worth of CDOs on their books causing massive losses, institution failures, and bringing the U.S. financial system to the brink of collapse. The U.S. government injected over $700 billion into the financial system to prevent what was expected to be the greatest financial calamity the world had ever seen.

While there are many components of Dodd–Frank those listed below are some of the key provisions with an explanation of how each worked:

- Creation of the Financial Stability Oversight Council
- Creation of the Consumer Financial Protection Bureau
- The Volcker Rule

- Creation of the SEC Office of Credit Ratings
- Creation of a whistleblower program

The Financial Stability Oversight Council was tasked with identifying risks to the U.S. financial system, particularly the potential failure of financial firms deemed critical to the financial system and/or being "too big to fail." According to the U.S. Department of Treasury, the Financial Stability Oversight Council "provides for the first time, comprehensive monitoring of the stability of our nation's financial system" by "promoting market discipline and responding to emerging risks to the stability of the United States financial system" (Financial Stability Oversight Council 2020). As such, the Financial Stability Oversight Council, in conjunction with the Orderly Liquidation Authority, have the power to liquidate or restructure financial companies as needed.

The Consumer Financial Protection Bureau was created to prevent predatory lending to individuals deemed "risky." The theory was that a major contributing factor to the 2008 financial crisis was the ease at which risky borrowers or "subprime" borrowers were able to secure mortgages to purchase a home. These borrowers were sold complicated mortgages and could not keep up with the payments resulting in exorbitantly high default rates. In response, the Consumer Financial Protection Bureau forced mortgage lenders to use simple language in loan agreements and curbed the commissions received on higher fee loans or loans that would generate more revenue for the bank.

The Volcker Rule is more complicated and requires some historical perspective. The Glass–Stegall Act of 1933 limited a bank's capabilities by separating banking services from investment and brokerage services. However, in 1999, the Graham–Leach Bliley Act repealed much of the Glass–Stegall act, making it possible for banks to engage in commercial banking activities as well as investment banking and securities trading. After the 2008 financial crisis, the Volcker Rule looked to put more safeguards in place.

Some of the safeguards in the Volcker Rule include "banks can no longer trade securities, derivatives, commodities future, and options for their own account. This is called proprietary trading. It limits their investment in, and relationships with hedge funds or private equity funds" (Amadeo

2020). It also mandates that CEOs of financial corporations attest in writing each year that their firm is in compliance with the Volcker Rule. Ultimately, the Volcker Rule prevents banks from using their own money to make risky investments, lowering the probability that another huge, federally funded bailout will be needed.

The creation of the SEC Office of Credit Ratings was intended to provide oversight of rating agencies known as "nationally recognized statistical rating organizations" (NRSROs) (Jessica Kane 2020) that provide assessments of financial products such as mortgages. A contributor of the 2008 financial crisis was the inflated ratings on mortgages by rating agencies based on little or no information. The SEC Office of Credit Ratings is now tasked with examining, monitoring, and issuing guidance to NRSROs to ensure the rating agencies themselves are providing accurate, reliable information so as to clearly identify the risk associated with the rated assets.

The creation of the whistleblower program in the Dodd–Frank regulation highlighted two things: (1) financially compensates a "whistleblower" (someone who provides information of criminality or wrongdoing) for voluntarily providing information about a violation of law and leads to a successful enforcement action and (2) protected the whistleblower from retaliation as a result of sharing his or her concerns. Retaliation against and the protection of a whistleblower's identity has garnered national attention in the United States after a "whistleblower" report initiated an investigation into the president for colluding with Russia. Whether the situation is financially based or not, the protections afforded to whistleblowers continues to be debated in the U.S. legal system.

Summary

The U.S. financial system is a vast, complex network of regulatory agencies who monitor, examine, and create financial regulations. They are the first line of defense against any internal or external threat to the U.S. financial system. Right behind those regulators and regulations are the financial institutions themselves who must quickly, efficiently, and accurately respond to those regulations. The response by financial institutions should be ongoing, comprehensive training programs that focus on improving the understanding of, monitoring of, detecting of, and thwarting of any internal or external threats to the financial system. It is also up to the regulators and banks to ensure the customers of these institutions are well informed of applicable rules and regulations to protect the assets in which they trust these institutions with. Lastly, there is a tremendous opportunity in the United States and across the globe for secondary institutions to offer programs geared to the legalities, implications, and execution of adequate compliance procedures since the financial world continually becomes more and more complex. There will never be a time in history where the banking system no longer needs oversight and governance, but the joint efforts of the regulators, regulations, banks, employees, customers, and education institutions can provide a safe, reliable, and efficient financial system that aids the domestic and world economy.

CHAPTER 9

The Future

AI Projects in Banking

"Artificial Intelligence" (AI) and "digitization" are two of the hottest buzz words when discussing advancements in banking technology. According to Investopedia, AI "refers to the simulation of human intelligence in machines that are programmed to think and act like humans" (Frankenfield 2020) and digitization is the convergence of data, in this case banking data, to a digital format that is used to provide products and services to end users. While AI and digitization are common terms in today's discussions about advancements in banking technology, discussions of AI originated in 1956 when the term was first coined by a computer and cognitive scientist named John McCarthy. Progress in AI applications was up and down for the next 40 years until research ramped up in the early 1990s. Fast forward to today and AI, along with digitization of data, has far-reaching applications in areas of health care, manufacturing, farming, security and surveillance, and financial services, to name a few.

This chapter will focus on the different ways AI is being used and how it has impacted the banking industry.

The Impact on AI in the Banking Industry

AI is being used in the front, middle, and back offices of banks and financial institutions in many ways including, but not limited to automating tasks, customer service, fraud detection and prevention, and securities trading. Numerous sources cite the effectiveness and impact AI is having and will continue to have in the banking industry with some cost savings estimates reaching into the trillions of dollars by 2030. A 2018 estimate of the "business value" of AI in banking "including the cost savings and efficiencies of introducing AI technology compared to keeping existing infrastructure and processes" (Banks to Invest $300 Billion in AI by 2030; 2019) was $41.1 billion and expected to rise to $300 billion by 2030.

With banks investing more heavily in AI technology, it is naturally anticipated that banks will experience significant efficiencies in its processes resulting in the loss of jobs for employees. One estimate by Wells Fargo indicates that increases in the usage of AI in banking will eliminate as many as 200,000 jobs over the next 10 years (Kelly 2019). Employees that are most likely to be impacted will be those whose jobs are manual and repetitive, including tellers, customer service representatives, and those who investigate fraudulent activity.

The next section will look at the different ways banks are using AI technology.

Natural Language Processing

While there are many branches of AI, banks are using two specific branches: natural language processing and machine learning. With natural language processing, AI software converts speech into sounds and words, words into sounds, and analyzes those sounds to determine what was most likely said. However, it does not always have to be sounds. Natural language processing can also simulate conversations via text message, mobile applications, and even websites to produce a human-like interaction. The natural language processor is most likely a type of "chatbot" that can interface with the user by talking or typing and the user may not even know it is actually a chatbot doing the work and not a real human being.

To get a better understanding of how AI natural language processing works, the below is an excerpt from a 2018 article from Relinns that explains exactly how Amazon's Alexa, one of the most recognizable natural language processors, works:

- "Alex bot first records your speech and interprets sounds
- The recording of your speech is sent to Amazon's servers to be analyzed
- The servers breakdown whatever you said into sounds

- It then consults a database containing vast data and information to find which words closely correspond to the combination of individual sounds
- Then, Amazon's bot identifies key words to make sense of the task and carry out the corresponding functions
- Amazon sends the information back to your device and Alexa may speak; if Alexa needs to say anything back to you, it would go through the same process above but in reverse order" (Is Amazon Alexa a Chatbot? 2008).

The premise is the same for other natural language processing applications—breaking words into sounds, sounds into patterns, analyzing those patterns, and responding or taking some kind of action step.

The banking industry used natural language processing mainly in various customer contact points to improve customer service. Whether you are calling into a customer service area via telephone, sending a text message, interfacing with a named AI application (for example, Bank of America's AI interface is named, "Erica") or communicating online via "chat," the initial interface uses natural language processing to understand the speech or command. One example is when someone calls into a customer service area via telephone. The voice response system will instruct the caller to "say or enter the account number using your touch tone telephone." If the person speaks their account number, the natural language processor can recognize the numbers and letters provided to access account details. Once the account is verified, the system will provide a menu of options to choose from including balance information, recent activity, or to speak to a representative. Depending on the choices the customer makes, the system will also provide the ability to conduct simple tasks such as transfer money, change a PIN on a card, or order a replacement card.

Natural language processing is also used to resolve customer issues. For example, a customer may access his account online and discovers that he was inadvertently charged twice for an online purchase. Already on his bank's website, he clicks on the "chat now" box and would automatically be connected to a natural language processor or chatbot. The chatbot would type on the screen, "How can I help you?" and the customer may type a basic response such as "dispute a charge." The chatbot can recognize that issue and provide a selection of recent activity the customer may wish to dispute. The chatbot will then go through the full process of taking the information, disputing the charge as a duplicate charge, and provide the customer with resolution information such as "Please be advised it will take up to 48 hours to credit your account." All these functions can be accomplished without any amount of human interaction or intervention.

What is absolutely critical about having natural language processors perform these basic tasks though is to have people on standby to resolve complex issues or respond to complex inquiries. For example, a chatbot would not be able to resolve a problem where a person says they entered an online trade to purchase a stock at a limit price of $100 but the system executed the trade at $101. That is a complicated problem that would require research, thought, and analysis, something that a chatbot would not be able to do with the technology that exists today. As such, the need for human resource personnel may be declining, but it will be a long time from now before they go away for good, if ever.

Machine Learning

The branch of machine learning in AI technology has far more possibilities for banks to harness than that of natural language processing. Banks are using machine learning in areas of fraud detection, investment predictions, document processing, money laundering prevention, and marketing to name a few.

A great description of what machine learning is can be found in an article written by Karen Hao for *MIT Technology Review*, which describes machine learning as, "Machine learning algorithms use statistics to find patterns in massive amounts of data. And data, here, encompasses a lot of things—numbers, words, images, clicks, what you have. If it can be digitally stored, it can be fed into a machine learning algorithm" (Hao 2018). The machine learning algorithm then analyzes all of that data, recognizes patterns in the data that humans cannot easily determine, and then applies that data for identifying anomalies, making predictions, and creating content.

The below reviews some key applications of machine learning used by banks.

Fraud Detection

Banks are currently using a combination of "supervised" and "unsupervised" machine learning in their fraud detection and prevention efforts. Supervised machine learning uses a set of inputs and outputs that the machine "learns" from by mapping an input to an output. The machine will analyze numerous iterations of inputs to outputs until it can accurately predict the output when a new input is introduced.

For example, a bank may input hundreds of thousands of transactions where some are legitimate and some are fraud. The supervised machine learning process will learn which ones are legitimate while others are fraudulent, progressing to the point where if the bank asked the machine to analyze one more transaction, it could predict with a high degree of certainty whether or that transaction was legitimate or fraudulent.

Unsupervised learning on the other hand is where there is an input but no output. The machine does not learn and is left to devise and present the data in its own way. Unsupervised machine learning is good for understanding "clustering" (understanding groups of data such as customers by purchasing power) and "association" (commonalities in data such as customers that purchase both X and Y). (Brownlee 2016).

Banks apply an integrated approach of both supervised and unsupervised machine learning to look at large sets of data, realize clusters or associations of data, and machines learn with a high degree of certainty if an individual transaction is legitimate or fraud in a matter of milliseconds. As more transactions are used in the supervised learning process, the model becomes a better predictor of legitimate or fraudulent transactions, saving banks and customers billions of dollars annually.

Investment Predictions

Everyday financial advisors around the world listen to economic data to predict which stocks, sectors, and geographical regions provide the best opportunity for investment. There are existing models that use a risk-based approach to determine what mix of investments are best suited for an individual or a company, and then which investments within the universe of investments are best suited to reach the goals of the person or company. As such, it may be difficult to understand or buy into how and why AI models are being used to make investment predictions when there seems to be a saturated technology market already capable of making such decisions. Enter the world of AI for investment decision making.

AI machine learning to make investment decisions starts with large amounts of data—current economic data, forecasted economic data, making associations of economic data on price changes on individual investments, sectors of investments, or geography-specific investments, data that relates to overall market sentiment, and the ability to "analyze" reports that may point to which direction an investment can go in. Again, the more data this is applied, the more the machine learns, the better it will understand how all of these factors relate to one another and can make predictions about how investments will play out. This type of data analysis is impossible to be replicated by humans and cannot be replicated by hard-coded programs. Only AI programs that have the ability to ingest a large amount of data, map inputs to outputs, make associations, and learn from them are capable of making more accurate predictions.

The question then becomes how do banks use the information generated from machine learning applications to make investment decisions. One example is that banks could use these applications to assist an individual customer make decisions about what to invest in, how much to invest in, and what to expect from the return of the prescribed portfolio taking into consideration variable such as risk tolerance, investment time horizon, expected portfolio performance and marry that with past, present, and future economic conditions, geopolitical conditions, negative news, and other cautionary details that could impact performance.

Another way banks are using AI for investment decisions is for asset managers to review AI predictions for "bias." As data is analyzed by an AI machine learning application, it makes associations and clusters that may or may not be accurate. This could be due to poor construction of the algorithm or the machine's "learning process" but asset management teams will employ data scientists to determine if a level of bias exists. If so, the data scientists will introduce new data and manipulate existing data to improve the overall predictions of the machine. Overall, this greatly improves the quality of data analysis and when coupled with human cognition, the results are markedly improved.

Document Processing

Traditionally, document review, classification, analysis, and processing in banking was a manual, time-consuming, costly process that could only be carried out by bank personnel. As the digitization of information (the conversion of hard and soft copy information into "electronic" information) has evolved considerably, so too has the ability to automatically recreate the same process without human intervention. It is through the use of AI machine learning that makes this possibility a reality.

According to an article by Sophia Brook, there are five main stages to AI document processing:

1. Importing data into the system
2. Data classification, tagging, indexing
3. Optical character recognition
4. Correct interpretation of symbols, in context
5. Decision making (Brooke 2019)

When importing data into the machine learning system, it is important that the machine be able to read different types of data in different formats and extract it accordingly. Data could be in the form of a PDF, handwritten, Microsoft application, report, chart, a spreadsheet, and so on, but the information should be readable and extractable in order to synthesize it and classify it as part of step two.

Step two involves data classification. This means the system needs to be able to differentiate between data types and classifications, for example, a person's name versus a corporate name or dollar amounts of transactions versus security values. The machine learning application will not be able to move forward until all extracted data is classified, tagged, and indexed accordingly.

The next step in document processing is optical character recognition. This is the process of looking at the classified, tagged, and indexed data and organizing it in such a way that is easily readable by machines and by humans. This makes it easier for document review in case there are errors in the assimilation of data.

Step four involves ensuring that symbols have been interpreted by the system correctly. Symbols include characters such as commas, dots, dollar signs, percentages, among other symbols. The system must be able to differentiate between these symbols and apply logic correctly to ensure data calculations and data interpretations are accurate.

Lastly, the system should be able to make decisions. For example, if the system is designed for automatic payment of an invoice, the system must be able use the invoice as an input, have the data classified correctly, read the information, interpret the symbols correctly, understand how much the payment is for, and process the payment. This can all be done using AI machine learning technology but is highly dependent on how the application was designed and performs as it is intended.

Money Laundering Prevention

It should be well understood by now that AI machine learning application involves at a basic level data input and analysis. One way that banks are utilizing these capabilities is to prevent money laundering. As you can imagine large data sets of transactions are fed into the AI machine learning tool with both legitimate transactions and laundered transactions. As the machine learning tool makes associations between the different characteristics of both legitimate and laundered transactions, it can predict with greater accuracy if a transaction should be reviewed or not. This is critical in the process of reducing "false positives."

False-positives are transactions that have been flagged for some reason but are actually legitimate transactions. When a false-positive is identified, the bank analyst does not know the transaction is a false-positive until he or she invests a significant amount of time researching the transaction. This process is ineffective in two ways: (i) the time it takes to review one transaction is quite lengthy and (ii) reviewing transactions that turn out to be false-positives prevents the analyst from reviewing otherwise a true positive hit.

A reduction in false-positives could be accomplished by improving the existing algorithms using a neural network. It works by taking the false-positives, feeding them back into the machine learning tool, and having the algorithms make adjustments in the algorithm logic to get better at identifying true positive transactions. Some estimates predict that using AI machine learning in the money laundering prevention process could reduce false-positive rates by as much as 98 percent.

Marketing

Have you ever noticed that you start receiving advertisements for products or services after mentioning it on a social media site, out loud in the presence of a "smart device" such as Amazon's Alexa, or did a search for that product or service on Google? If so, that is because machine learning tools are following your every step to understand your interests, your buying habits, your location, and other information to market products and services to you that the cyberworld has determined you want or need. This is because of machine learning in marketing.

Obtaining the data is only part of the equation though. Banks and other organizations are then using that data to make very personal recommendations to you based on your "electronic profile." For example, if you are in the market for a new car, maybe you get marketing information for all different types of cars from different car manufacturers. However, when a machine learning tool can incorporate information such as job, salary, geographical location, number of family members, Internet searches, pictures liked on dealership sites, et cetera, car manufacturers can now provide information on specific car models, colors, prices, and nearby locations to where you can shop. This information is obviously a powerful tool when demonstrating a company's product suite, be it a car manufacturer or a bank.

Conclusion

There is no doubt that improvements in bank technology will largely come from advancements in AI in the forms of natural language processing and machine learning. Banks will be able to provide tailored customer service, improve efficiencies, detect and deter fraud, identify money laundering other types of nefarious financial schemes, and market-specific products and services to those most interested in them. It will require hearty financial investments upfront with a windfall of money saved later. And lastly, it is expected a number of jobs will be lost in the banking industry over the coming decade but to what extent is unknown.

CHAPTER 10

Top Strategies for Call Center Management

Call centers at major banks 25 years ago were large, open spaces with rows and rows of employees, all wearing wired headsets, taking calls related to debit card charges, balance inquiries, check clearing activity, wire transfers, direct deposits, and in some cases, basic information regarding their investments such as stock quotes and recent dividend payments. The Internet was in its infancy stages and CD-ROMs were sent to clients to load the program onto their computer for enhanced services after paying an enrollment fee. Calls came in one after the other nonstop throughout the day, creating a high stress environment with a large percentage of employee turnover every year. A call center employee was evaluated on quality of the call based on the level of service provided, the accuracy of information given, and the number of phone calls taken each day as there were prescribed metrics that determined what the "average" length of a call should be. Those who persevered in that environment were elevated to assistant supervisor and supervisor roles, which came with the benefit of no longer being "tied to a headset." Employee compensation was low, bonuses were measly, and it was hard to argue against as call centers were basically "cost" centers that some perceived as a necessary component of the business model that was not "sexy," "appealing," or "noteworthy" to launch a career in business from.

Over time, call centers have gotten smaller, more efficient, and more personalized, warehousing a treasure trove of invaluable information that when used properly, becomes a source of sustained customer growth and satisfaction. A highly efficient call center is the "glue" that creates a "sticky" relationship with each client, providing excellent service, offering bundled products or services, and leveraging available information to create a complete financial package specific to each customers' needs or wants. The products or services consumed by a customer makes for the sticky relationship, providing discounts and perks with each new product or service added. In the end, the bank will be a one-stop-shop for all financial products and services for the customer. It all starts with a well-seasoned relationship manager and then capitalizing on call center opportunities to strengthen customer relationships.

This chapter will look at the top strategies employed for managing a call center of today and the impact it has on the overall financial institution.

Call Center Management: Where to Begin

Presume you are a new call center manager in an already established call center. You are known as an energetic leader, good with employees, and able to achieve results but the call center has not produced the results the company has expected and is looking for you to turn it around. Welcome to your new role! Now, the most important question is where to begin.

Just as in any other business situation requiring a turnaround, first a foremost, the manager must have a strategy for how to approach the situation. As such, the first question that needs to be answered is, "What is the best strategy to use to manage the call center?" As referenced earlier in this book, It is critical to distinguish between a strategy and goals, making sure you indeed have a strategy. Expanding on Ann Latham's review of what a strategy is, she says, "A strategic framework must establish what the organization will do to deliver value for which customers are willing to pay and how it expects to hit target revenues and profits" (Latham 2017). Applying that statement to the problem of managing a call center, a call center manager can then decide what his or her organization will do to deliver value and hit target revenues.

The next logical question to figure out is what problem or problems exist in the call center. If the manager wants to make a real impact, they must do a deep dive into each component of the call center. Components of call center management process include, but are not limited to the quality of the employees, the training programs for those employees, the call center culture, the performance metrics that measure various aspects of call center performance, the technology used within the call center to enhance customer service, assist with scheduling, and providing metrics, vendor relations, and budgeting. While all of these components of call center management require significant thought and investigation to get to the grassroots of any issues, leading to the starting point for implementing corrective actions, let's first look at one of the most valuable call center resources: its employees.

Call Center Employees

Hiring call center employees starts with the recruitment process. As such, the call center manager should be recruiting people who are younger, preferably not having worked in a professional environment before, have a good personality, display good emotional intelligence, a willingness to learn, and are "coachable." The reason for hiring those that fit this mold is that it increases the likelihood that the person can be taught the skills needed to be successful and more likely to stay versus someone who may not look at a customer service role positively and contaminating the work environment.

Once the right employee is identified, the bank should provide a top-of-the-line training program that provides the right balance of classroom and on-the-job training. This requires having a great training staff and a pool of on-the-job mentors who display all the desired behaviors a great call center employee should have including providing exceptional customer service, multitasking, following up on open issues, and communicating in a clear, concise manner. Having exposure to classroom training and then applying that knowledge on-the-job with a trusted mentor helps lay the solid foundation the new employee needs to be successful in the future. Success though is dependent on many factors, maybe none more important than the call center culture.

Call Center Culture

Once the call center manager feels the right employees are in place, it is critical that the culture matches the strategy of what the firm is willing to do to achieve service and financial goals. It is well understood that one of the main goals of a call center is to provide excellent customer service, but the call center manager cannot neglect the employees themselves. As such, the culture should be both customer-centric *and* employee-friendly. Call centers that are customer-centric are ones that empower employees, use customer feedback to improve service, provide targeted feedback for each employee on areas to improve service, linking customer service performance to management objectives, having management continually echo the importance for excellent customer service, and (this is a big one that is often overlooked) linking front line customer service teams to the back office operational teams that support the service area. This means that if you have people in the call center telling customers to expect something to happen in 24 hours, the back office operational areas can achieve that task. So many times, particularly in large financial institutions, there is a major disconnect between the front line call center and back office operational areas that the end-to-end customer service experience falls short of expectations. It is often difficult to figure out exactly where the bottleneck is when these shortcomings take place so the best thing to do is make sure both the front line and back office operations are in sync right from the beginning. Any changes to policies or procedures should be communicated to all support areas to stay in sync going forward.

Regarding the characteristics that make for an employee-friendly culture, those could include anything that makes employees feel happy, valued, satisfied with their job, and looking forward to future employment opportunities. While many creative ideas such as providing free coffee and snacks, having a meaningful reward system in place, or sponsoring fun team building events could make the culture seem employee-friendly, the best thing you can do is talk to your employees and ask them what would make them feel valued. Getting information from your employees completely removes the risk of guessing what you think will make them feel valued and getting right to the heart of what will actually make them feel valued. Plus, there is the added benefit of including the employees in the process, making them feel empowered and that their voices matter. This instills confidence in management and translates into a positive, productive employee culture.

One of the great benefits of having an employee-friendly culture is an increase in employee retention. The national average rate of call center employee turnover in the United States is estimated to be anywhere from 30 to 45 percent. (High Turnover is Costing Call Centers: Why Employee Retention Should be a Priority and What to do About it 2020). The cost to replace an employee is estimated to be as high as 50 percent of the employee's salary so there is plenty of motivation on the side of the bank to do the best it can to retain employees. When surveying employees who have stayed with a company, oftentimes one of the main drivers is the company culture whereas the opposite is true for employees who leave a company citing a poor company culture (and lack of pay) for leaving the company.

Hiring the right employees and creating a client centric and employee culture are huge accomplishments in and of themselves, but there's more to do. The next step a call center manager should take is to look at metrics and understand the story those metrics are telling.

Call Center Metrics

There are two critical factors to understand when considering call center metrics: deciding what to measure and then taking action based on those measurements. Shauna Geraghty provides a framework that will help any call center manager select the appropriate KPIs to consider in a 10-step process outlined below:

1. Identify KPIs that reflect your business objectives and corporate strategy.
2. Accurately define KPIs.
3. Establish how the KPI will be calculated.
4. Define each KPI's purpose.
5. Ensure the KPIs are measuring different domains.
6. Set performance targets for each KPI.
7. Define execution steps for each target.
8. Develop an action plan if the KPI doesn't meet the target.
9. Continually review KPIs.
10. Refine KPIs when necessary (Geraghty 2013).

Typical call center management metrics include service level (how many calls are answered in specified period of time, usually measured within seconds), call abandoned rate (how many calls are dropped because the customer did not wait long enough to get assistance), average handle time (how long an average call lasts), first call resolution (was the customer service agent able to resolve the customer issue with one call or is further follow-up necessary), and lastly, how much time is spent on follow-up (research time required to resolve complicated customer issues that takes the agent off the phone). These metrics are a good starting place to understand how well service is being provided to your customers.

Using the aforementioned metrics as the foundation for call center performance, how the call center manager addresses deficiencies in these processes could go in many different directions. For example, if service levels are low, is it because of poor employee productivity or is the agent scheduling software deficient in identifying peak call times and could be resolved by adding staff at certain times throughout the day. If the abandoned call rate is high, is it because there are too many calls coming into your call center or is the automated service menu deficient putting callers into endless loops they cannot get out of and just decide to hang up. Once the call center manager is able to determine the true root cause of these metrics, action should be taken. As Geraghty points out though, KPIs should be continually reviewed and refined to ensure that the right measurements are being taken along with appropriate action steps.

The call center of today does more than take phone calls though; it also answers emails and live chats as part of the customer service experience. These channels provide an additional touchpoint to interact with customers so it is important to understand the dynamics of these touchpoints, making sure they are part of the KPI analytics and associated action steps.

When answering chats, the first response time is a key metric to be reviewed. The metric is measured by calculating how long a customer had to wait before an agent's initial response to the chat. Another key metric used when evaluating chat service performance is average resolution time, similar to average handle time for a phone agent. It calculates how long it takes an agent to close the conversation. Similarly to a telephone-based call center, there are also chat metrics such as missed chats, first contact resolution rate, and customer service feedback that are all used to understand the client experience.

One important note regarding chats in banking is that not all chats are used for resolving customer inquiries; chats are also used by clients and potential clients looking for information on products and services offered through the bank. Therefore, looking at conversion chat metrics, the rate at which an agent converts a chat to a "sale" may also be a way of looking at employee performance and customer satisfaction. The point here is that how the call center is structured (phone only, phone and chats, etc.) and what the objectives of the call center are (service only, service and sales, etc.) will drive the metrics used to evaluate performance and assist the call center manager make decisions of how to improve performance.

Call Center Technology

When reviewing call center technology, the call center manager should be cognizant that any good call center technology is one that helps the call center achieve the goals and objectives of the organization, In a call center environment, this usually equates to enhanced customer service and satisfaction. As such, this paper will focus on three areas of call center technology that do just that: creating a well-designed interactive voice response (IVR) system, artificial intelligence and machine learning, and cloud-based contact centers that will ultimately create a robust call center experience, all contributing to an elevated level of customer satisfaction.

Anyone who is reading this chapter undoubtedly experienced calling a customer service area where the IVR system gives what seems to be an endless number of options to say or choose from, interwoven with marketing information that prolongs actually speaking to someone, getting caught in an endless loop of options as none of the options provided seem to be the right ones, or even better, the IVR system cannot understand what you are saying and does not provide a touchtone option as an alternative. All the while, your blood pressure skyrockets and your satisfaction level plummets, resulting in a very poor customer experience.

The problem with this type of IVR is not the technology itself but how the technology is applied. An effective IVR is one that is simple, allows for pauses so people can speak or enter in their responses, provides instructions only when an error is made, and always (seriously, always) provides the opportunity to speak to a customer service agent. This will provide for a better customer experience and flips the blood pressure and satisfaction levels in the other direction.

The use of artificial intelligence (AI) in the banking industry was discussed in the previous chapter, but the applications of AI, particularly natural language processing and machine learning are essential in call center management. The use of natural language processing applications allows the system to recognize both spoken and written communication as well as responding by a system generated voice or in writing or text. Systems that can understand natural language provide more opportunities for the customer to execute self-service options, completely negating the need for a customer service agent. Self-service options can be anything from conducting basic transactions, ordering documents or marketing information, or receiving automated account updates.

Machine learning on the other hand can do things like recognize patterns in customer behavior, including knowing where they shop, what their risk tolerance levels are, what question they ask most often, and tailor service specific to that customer. Really good banking call centers will also use machine learning technology to offer products and services specific to the client based on analyzed data that makes for a better customer experience. Again, all of this is done without the intervention of a customer service agent but provides very high levels of service and equally, customer satisfaction.

Machine learning can also be used to form patterns in call center activity that highlight when clients call in, the most common problems your customers are facing, how long it takes to resolve those problems, and what potential solutions could be used to solve those problems. As such, it is important to note that there are both customer-facing and noncustomer-facing applications of AI that could improve call center performance.

The last component of call center technology this chapter will look at is cloud-based applications. Many existing call centers run on old, legacy systems that make it difficult to add new customer contact points (text, email, social media) or extract meaningful metrics regarding customer service issues and solutions. A cloud-based contact center on the other hand is Internet-based and provides flexible solutions that are easily adaptable and more reliable than legacy systems.

For example, if you were to call into a legacy system based call center, the IVR may not be dynamic, you may get through to an agent only to be transferred to the agent that originally took your call, and you would most likely not have the ability to communicate in a way other than telephone and email. Contrarily, if you called into a cloud-based call center, the IVR would be highly in tune with your account and the products and services you most often use, the agent taking your call would be able to access all of your previous interactions with other agents and pick up from where he or she left off, and you would have the ability to chat via text, chatbot, phone, or email, whichever was more convenient for you. A cloud-based call center is also scalable and fluid that can adapt to things like an increase in your customer base or material changes in client preferences. Overall, the cloud-based center provides more opportunities to provide better service to the customer.

Conclusion

Managing a call center is no easy task as many facets of the business need to be considered. Everything from hiring the right employees, creating the right culture, understanding and taking corrective actions based on call center metrics, and leveraging technology to improve customer service and overall efficiency is a daunting challenge for the most seasoned professional. However, having a strategy to tackle the problem is the best place to start.

References

A Guide to the Project Management Body of Knowledge (PMBOK Guide) 5th Addition. 2013. Newton Square, Pennsylvania: Project Management Institute, Inc.

About the Fed. 2020. Retrieved from Federal Reserve: https://federalreserve.gov/aboutthefed.htm

Amadeo, K. July 23, 2020. "The Volcker Rule and How it Protects You." Retrieved from the Balance https://thebalance.com/volcker-rule-summary-3305905

AML Software. 2020. Retrieved from Capterra Inc, https://capterra.com/aml-software/

Anderson, R. n.d. "rickanderson2managementinfotainer." Retrieved from the Management Infotainer, https://rickanderson2managementinfotainer.wordpress.com/2014/06/25/world-war-1-and-the-gantt-chart/

Bank Secrecy Act. 2020. Retrieved from FDIC.gov, www.fdic.gov/regulations/safety/manual/section8-1.pdf

Bank Secrecy Act, Anti-Money Laundering, and Office of Foreign Assets Control. 2020. Retrieved from fdic.gov, https://fdic.gov/regulations/safety/manual/section8-1.pdf

Banks to Invest $300 Billion in AI by 2030. April 16, 2019. Retrieved from Markets Media, https://marketsmedia.com/banks-to-invest-300-billion-in-ai-by-2030/

Beattie, A. May 9, 2020. "How the Federal Reserve was Formed." Retrieved from Investopedia.com, https://investopedia.com/articles/economics/08/federal-reserve.asp

Blueprint Agile Methodologies. 2020. Retrieved from blueprintsys, http://blueprintsys.com/agile-development-101/agile-methodologies

Brooke, S. October 3, 2019. "Why AI is the Next Step in Document Processing." Retrieved from Heartbeat https://heartbeat.fritz.ai/why-ai-is-the-next-step-in-document-processing-1941785c5425

Brownlee, J. March 16, 2016. "Machine Learning Mastery, Supervised and Unsupervised Machine Algorithms." Retrieved from Machine Learning Mastery, https://machinelearningmastery.com/supervised-and-unsupervised-machine-learning-algorithms/

BSA Compliance and Section 314. 2020. Retrieved from Comply Advantage https://complyadvantage.com/knowledgebase/usa-patriot-act/

CFPB Consumer Financial Protection Bureau. 2020. Retrieved from Consumer Finance https://consumerfinance.gov/about-us/the-bureau/

Chiu, Y.C. 2010. *An Introduction to the History of Project Management from the Earliest Times to A.D. 1900.* The Netherlands: Eburon Academic Publishers.

Consumer Financial Protection Bureau. n.d. "Retrieved from Consumer Finance." https://consumerfinance.gov/about-us/the-bureau/creatingthebureau/

Curule, J. 1994–1995. "The Money Laundering Control Act of 1986." Retrieved from scholarship.law.nd.edu, https://scholarship.law.nd.edu/law_faculty_scholarship/21/

Dalcher, D., Prof. April 2017. "What has Taylor Ever Done for us? Scientific and Humane Management Reconsidered." *PM World Journal* 6, no. 4, 1–11. Retrieved from www.pmworldjournal.net

Eby, K. July 29, 2016. "Comprehensive Guide to the Agile Manifesto." Retrieved from smartsheet.com, http://smartsheet.com/comprehensive-guide-values-principles-agile-manifesto

Federal Reserve Education. 2020. Retrieved from Federal Reserve https://federalreserveeducation.org/about-the-fed/structure-and-functions

Financial Stability Oversight Council. 2020. Retrieved from U.S. Department of Treasury https://home.treasury.gov/policy-issues/financial-markets-financial-institutions-and-fiscal-service/fsoc

Fines for Banks that Breached U.S. OFAC Sanctions. 2020. Retrieved from refinitiv.com, https://refinitiv.com/content/dam/marketing/en_us/documents/infographics/fines-for-banks-that-breached-us-sanctions-infographic.pdf; photo originally sourced from http://treasury.gov/resource-center/sanctions/CivPen/Pages/civpen-index2.aspxx

Founding of the OCC & the National Banking System. 2020. "Retrieved from Office of the Comptroller of the Currency." https://occ.gov/about/who-we-are/history/founding-occ-national-bank-system/index-founding-occ-national-banking-system.html

Frankenfield, J. March 13, 2020. "Artificial Intelligence (AI)." Retrieved from Investopedia, https://investopedia.com/terms/a/artificial-intelligence-ai.asp

Gantt, H.L. 1919. *Works, Wages, and Profits.* New York: The Engineering Magazine Co. https://mosaicprojects.com.au/Gantt/workwagesprofits.pdf

Geraghty, S. January 16, 2013. "10 Steps to Select Optimal KPIs to Monitor Performance." Retrieved from https://talkdesk.com/blog/10-steps-to-select-optimal-kpis-to-monitor-call-center-performance/

Giannantonio, C.M., and A.E. Hurley-Hanson. 2011. "Frederick Winslow Taylor: Reflections on the Relevance of The Principles of Scientific Management 100 Years Later." *Journal of Business Management*, pp. 7–10.

Google. June 14, 2020. Retrieved from Google www.google.com

Hao, K. November 17, 2018. "What is Machine Learning." Retrieved from MIT Technology Review, https://technologyreview.com/2018/11/17/103781/what-is-machine-learning-we-drew-you-another-flowchart/

High Turnover is Costing Call Centers: Why Employee Retention Should be a Priority and What to do About it. 2020. Retrieved from CRM Gamified, https://crmgamified.com/turnover-in-call-centers-why-prioritize-employee-retention/

History of Anti-Money Laundering Laws. 2020. Retrieved from Financial Crimes Enforcement Network, https://fincen.gov/history-anti-money-laundering-laws

History-Biography. January 15, 2019. *history-biography.com*. Retrieved from history-biography.com, https://history-biography.com/henri-fayol/

Hugh McCulloch, the First Comptroller. 2020. Retrieved from Office of the Comptroller of the Currency, https://occ.gov/about/who-we-are/history/hugh-mcculloch-the-first-comptroller.html

ICA International Compliance Association. 2020. Retrieved from International Compliance Association https://int-comp.org/careers/your-career-in-compliance/what-is-compliance/

Is Amazon Alexa a Chatbot? November 16, 2008. Retrieved from Relinns Technology, https://relinns.com/blog/is-amazon-alexa-a-chatbot/

Jessica Kane, D.O. February 24, 2020. "The SEC's Office of Credit Ratings." Retrieved from SEC.gov, https://sec.gov/news/speech/speech-jessica-kane-2020-02-24

Joint Economic Committee. 2020. Retrieved from JEC.Senate.gov, https://.jec.senate.gov/public/_cache/files/20796f3c-cd05-422f-89f8-ec86f00a7577/consumer-protection-accomplishments-final 4-10-jw-lv-002-.pdf

Jon Wittwer, P. June 6, 2019. "Gantt Chart Template for Excel." Retrieved from vertex42, https://vertex42.com/ExcelTemplates/excel-gantt-chart.html

Kagan, J. May 11, 2020. "Federal Home Loan Bank Act." Retrieved from Investopedia: https://investopedia.com/terms/f/federal-home-loan-bank-act.asp

Kelly, J. October 8, 2019. "Wells Fargo Predicts that Robots will Steal 200,000 Banking Jobs Within the Next 10 Years." Retrieved from Forbes, https://forbes.com/sites/jackkelly/2019/10/08/wells-fargo-predicts-that-robots-will-steal-200000-bankng-jobs-within-the-next-10-years/#2869c3ec68d7

Kenton, W. April 19, 2019. "Office of Thrift Supervision." Retrieved from Investopedia, https://investopedia.com/terms/o/ots.asp

Kozak-Holland, M. 2011. *The History of Project Management*. Oshawa, ON, Canada: Multi-Media Publications Inc.

Kukreja, S. n.d. "Principles of Management by Henri Fayol." Retrieved from Management Study HQ, https://managementstudyhq.com/henri-fayol-principles-of-management.html

Larson, G. October 8, 2019. "Synthetic Identity Fraud is the Fastest Growing Financial Crime - What Can Banks Do to Fight It?" Retrieved from Forbes, https://forbes.com/sites/forbestechcouncil/2019/10/08/synthetic-identity-fraud-is-the-fastest-growing-financial-crime-what-can-banks-do-to-fight-it/#f4a12a7ecbe2

Latham, A. October 29, 2017. "What the Heck is a Strategy Anyway." Retrieved from Forbes.com, https://forbes.com/sites/annlatham/2017/10/29/what-the-heck-is-a-strategy-anyway/#2ec0a0e77ed8

Latham, A. October 29, 2017. "What the Heck is a Strategy Anyway?" Retrieved from Forbes, https://forbes.com/sites/annlatham/2017/10/29/what-the-heck-is-a-strategy-anyway/#80a0b457ed84

Laumann, A. July 16, 2019. "The History of Anti-money Laundering." Retrieved from kroll.com, https://kroll.com/en/insights/publications/compliance-risk/history-anti-money-laundering-united-states

Luis Lugo, Director, and Alan Cooperman, Associate Director, Research. 2012. *The Global Religious Landscape.* Washington, D.C.: Pew Research Center, Religion and Public Life.

Marsh, E.R. 1975. "The Harmonograph of Karol Adamiecki." *The Academy of Management Journal,* pp. 358–364.

Morgan, M.S. 1997. "Money Laundering: The American Law and Its Global Influence." Retrieved from smu.edu, https://scholar.smu.edu/cgi/viewcontent.cgi?article=1699&context=lbra

Mueller, J.P. March 28, 2007. "Agile Definitions and Solutions." Retrieved from CIO.com, http://cio.com/article/2439443/agile-development-agile-programming-definition-and-solutions.html

National Credit Union Association: Historical Timeline. 2020. Retrieved from National Credit Union Association, https://ncua.gov/about-ncua/historical-timeline#1970s

Organization. 2020. Retrieved from Office of the Comptroller of the Currency, https://occ.gov/about/who-we-are/organizations/index-organization.html

Patriot Act. 2020. Retrieved from Wikipedia https://en.wikipedia.org/wiki/Patriot_Act#Title_I:_Enhancing_domestic_security_against_terrorism

Payne, K. July 16, 2020. "What is the National Credit Union Administration?" *Forbes,* Retrieved from https://forbes.com/advisor/banking/what-is-the-national-credit-union-administration/

Peterson, P. 1987. "Training and Development: the View of Henry L. Gantt (1861 to 1919)." *SAM Advanced Management Journal,* pp. 20–23.

Project Management Institute. 2013. *The High Cost of Low Performance: The Essential Role of Communications.* Newton Square: Project Management Institute Headquarters.

Richard Breese, O.C. 2020. "The Project Sponsor Role and Benefits Realisation: More than 'Just Doing the Day Job'." *International Journal of Project Management,* nos. 38/1, pp. 17–26.

Shuttleworth, M. July 10, 2017. "Project Schedule Planning: PERT vs. CPM."

Retrieved from Project Risk Manager https://project-risk-manager.com/blog/pert-vs-cpm/

Smartsheet. 2020. Retrieved from smartsheet.com, http://smartsheet.com/content-center/best-practices/project-management/project-management-guide/waterfall-methodology

Stackhouse, J. April 24, 2018. "What is the Bank Secrecy Act, and Why Does It Exist?" Retrieved from www.stlouisfed.org, https://stlouisfed.org/on-the-economy/2018/april/what-bank-secrecy-act-why-exist, Tuesday, April 24, 2018

Stephen, T. November 14, 2005. "OFAC Compliance Pose Significant Challenges." Retrieved from Compliance Week, https://complianceweek.com/patriot-act-ofac-compliance-pose-significant-challenges/6858.article

Structure of the Federal Reserve System. 2020. Retrieved from Federal Reserve, https://federalreserve.gov/aboutthefed/structure-federal-reserve-system.htm

Taylor, F.W. 1911. *The Principles of Scientific Management.* New York, NY, USA and London, UK: Harper & Brothers, LCCN.

The Role of the SEC. 2020. Retrieved from Investor.gov, investor.gov/introduction-investing/investing-basics/role-sec

Towne, H.R. 1886. "The Engineer as an Economist." *American Society of Mechanical Engineers*, 2. New York, NY: Academy of Management..

Tucker, A. October 9, 2008. "The Financial Panic of 1907: Running from History." Retrieved from smithsonianmag.com, https://smithsonianmag.com/history/the-financial-panic-of-1907-running-from-history-82176328/

U.S. Department of the Treasury: History. 2020. Retrieved from U.S. Department of the Treasury, https://treasury.gov/about/history/Pages/ots.aspx

U.S. Department of Treasury: History. n.d. Retrieved from U.S. Department of Treasury, https://treasury.gov/about/organizational-structure/offices/pages/office-of-foreign-assets-control.aspx

U.S. Department of Treasury: Mission. 2020. Retrieved from U.S. Department of Treasury, https://treasury.gov/about/organizational-structure/offices/pages/office-of-foreign-assets-control.aspx

Understanding the FDIC: Overview of History of the Federal Deposit Insurance Corporation. 2020. Retrieved from thebalance.com, https://thebalance.com/what-is-the-fdic-315786

Wren, D.A. 2011. "The Centennial of Frederick W. Taylor's The Principles of Scientific Management: A Retrospective Commentary." *Journal of Business Management* 17, no. 1, p. 13.

About the Author

Dan Bonner has over 25 years' experience in the financial services industry with expertise in project management, operations, and compliance. He obtained his MBA from Penn State University in 2004, a PMP certification in 2015, and is a Vice President, Data Privacy Officer in Group Financial Security U.S. for BNP Paribas.

Index

OTHER TITLES IN THE PORTFOLIO AND PROJECT MANAGEMENT COLLECTION

Timothy J. Kloppenborg, Xavier University, Editor

- *Successfully Achieving Strategy Through Effective Portfolio Management* by Frank Parth
- *HybridP3M* by Lukasz Rosinski
- *Be Agile Do Agile* by Vittal Anantatmula and Timothy J. Kloppenborg
- *Project-Led Strategic Management* by James Marion, John Lewis, and Tracey Richardson
- *Workplace Jazz* by Gerald J. Leonard
- *Stakeholder-led Project Management, Second Edition* by Louise M. Worsley
- *Hybrid Project Management* by Mark Tolbert and Susan Parente
- *A.G.I.L.E. Thinking Demystified* by Frank Forte
- *Design: A Business Case* by Brigitte Borja de Mozota and Steinar Valade-Amland
- *Discoveries Through Personal Agility* by Raji Sivaraman and Michal Raczka
- *Project Communications* by Connie Plowman and Jill Diffendal
- *Quantitative Tools of Project Management* by David L. Olson
- *The People Project Triangle* by Stuart Copeland and Andy Coaton
- *How to Fail at Change Management* by James Marion and John Lewis
- *Core Concepts of Project Management* by David L. Olson

Concise and Applied Business Books

The Collection listed above is one of 30 business subject collections that Business Expert Press has grown to make BEP a premiere publisher of print and digital books. Our concise and applied books are for...

- Professionals and Practitioners
- Faculty who adopt our books for courses
- Librarians who know that BEP's Digital Libraries are a unique way to offer students ebooks to download, not restricted with any digital rights management
- Executive Training Course Leaders
- Business Seminar Organizers

Business Expert Press books are for anyone who needs to dig deeper on business ideas, goals, and solutions to everyday problems. Whether one print book, one ebook, or buying a digital library of 110 ebooks, we remain the affordable and smart way to be business smart. For more information, please visit www.businessexpertpress.com, or contact sales@businessexpertpress.com.

www.ingramcontent.com/pod-product-compliance
Lightning Source LLC
Chambersburg PA
CBHW061334220326
41599CB00026B/5181